WHAT CAN A MAN BELIEVE?

By

BRUCE BARTON

AUTHOR OF

The Man Nobody Knows
The Book Nobody Knows

**THE BOBBS-MERRILL COMPANY
PUBLISHERS   INDIANAPOLIS**

Printed in the United States of America

PRINTED AND BOUND
BY BRAUNWORTH & CO., INC
BROOKLYN, NEW YORK

A LETTER FROM A MAN

THE morning mail of September 25, 1926, contained the following blunt letter from a friend. He is the father of two children and president of the largest business of its kind in the world.

"I have read your two books. I have also read another which is better than you ever thought of writing, the book of Job.

"There is a man I like. He speaks my language. He was successful in business; he had a nice property; he was a good father, and a first-class citizen, trying to do his best. What happened? Suddenly, for no good reason, he loses his property and his health. His wife turns against him, and the whole town regards him as an outcast, punished for some secret sin.

"Worst of all, three theologians come to comfort him with platitudes that Job knows are not true. He tells them so. He says there is no answer to the riddle of the universe; that the wicked get on just as well as the righteous; that, if anything, God gives the bad an even better run for their money, and that his own good record has brought him nothing but misery.

A LETTER FROM A MAN

" 'Man that is born of a woman is of few days, and full of trouble.

" 'He cometh forth like a flower, and is cut down: he fleeth also as a shadow, and continueth not.'

"I am like Job in being fairly prosperous. I am like him also in getting no satisfaction out of the arguments of the godly.

"I see certain men, whom I respect, who seem to have faith. It gives them a satisfaction that I envy. I should like to have such a faith. I should like my son to have it, and the young men in my business.

"But, like Job, I shall not be a party to the acceptance and dissemination of bunk. I'd rather take his wife's advice and 'curse God and die' than add anything to the current over-supply of superstition, fear, and outworn creeds.

"I should like to see a book written which would answer the following questions:

"1. Would the world be better or worse off if it should abolish religion?

"2. Has the church done more harm than good?

"3. Of the various religions now extant which is the best?

"4. What few simple things, if any, can a business man believe?

"5. If there is to be a 'faith of the future' what kind of a faith will it be?

A LETTER FROM A MAN

"If you will write such a book I will read it. If it meets the questions honestly I will give it to my son and to the younger men in my business. If it dodges the questions; if it tries to creep up behind my reason through the back door of my emotions, I will burn it up as I should any other germ carrier.

"Consider this letter an order for the first copy. The theologians may shoot you at sunrise, but these questions that I have asked are what we ordinary fellows want to know. And that, by the way, might be your title—we want to know!

"But no pretense, remember. No side-stepping in order to keep from offending this sect or that. I can forgive you if you make an honest effort and fail, but if you trot out any of the shop-worn stuff you lose one gentle reader forever."

CONTENTS

WHAT CAN A MAN BELIEVE?

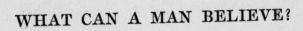

WHAT CAN A MAN BELIEVE?

CHAPTER I

SHOULD RELIGION BE ABOLISHED?

THE ship *l'Orient* carried a distinguished company of men upon an exciting errand that summer evening in 1798. The youth of twenty-eight, who had flamed across the sky of Europe like a comet, was on his way to greater glories.

"Europe is nothing but a mole hill," he exclaimed. "It is only in the Orient that there have been great empires and great revolutions, there where six hundred million people live."

So he was headed for Egypt to found an Oriental empire, and he was taking with him as helpers the best engineers and scientists of France.

On this evening he sat relaxed but interested, while the savants talked about religion. They said that while Egypt's religion had made its history, the religion itself was only myth and humbug. This was true of all religions. Dur-

ing certain phases in human development they
had their uses, but the time for them had long
since passed. There was no God, and men had
now reached a point where they could dare to
say it. Thus they argued, these scientists in
whom the spirit of atheistic revolt was so strong,
as it was rampant in all France at that hour.
And Napoleon leaned back and smiled and
listened. Finally he rose to leave them, and as
he did so he lifted his hand and pointed to the
stars that shone brilliantly through the deep
black sky.

"Very ingenious, Messieurs," he said, "but
who made all that?"

Here is another story, also about a warrior,
Captain Martin Scott, that famous crack-shot
of our southwestern frontier.

"I was once buffalo hunting in Arkansas,"
said the doughty captain. "I was on a strong,
well trained horse, pursuing a bull, when we
arrived at a rent or crack in the prairie, so wide
that it was necessary for the animals to leap it.
The bull went over first, and I, on the horse,
following it close, rose on my stirrups, craning a
little that I might perceive the width of the rent.
At that moment the bull turned round to charge;
the horse perceiving it, and knowing his
work, immediately wheeled also. This sudden
change of motion threw me off my saddle, and I

remained hanging by the side of the horse, with my leg over his neck. There I was, hanging on only by my leg, with my head downwards below the horse's belly. The bull rushed on to the charge, ranging up to the flank of the horse on the side where I was dangling, and the horse was so encumbered by my weight in that awkward position that each moment the bull gained upon him.

"At last my strength failed me; I felt that I could hold on but a few seconds longer; the head of the bull was close to me, and the steam from his nostrils blew into my face. I gave myself up for lost; all the prayer I could possibly call to mind at the time was the first two lines of a hymn I used to repeat as a child: 'Lord, now I lay me down to sleep'; and that I repeated two or three times, when, fortunately, the horse wheeled short round, evaded the bull, and leaped the gap. The jolt of the leap, after nearly dropping me into the gap, threw me up so high I gained the neck of the horse, and eventually my saddle. I then thought of my rifle and found that I had held it grasped in my hand during the whole time. I wheeled my horse and resumed the chase, and in a minute the bull was dead at my horse's feet."

It is a long jump from Napoleon to Captain Scott; what have two such dissimilar characters in common? Why link together two anecdotes so seemingly unrelated?

WHAT CAN A MAN BELIEVE?

Both stories are illustrations of the same curious fact. In every human being, whether emperor or cowboy, prince or pauper, philosopher or slave, there is a mysterious *something* which he neither understands nor controls. It may lie dormant for so long as to be almost forgotten; it may be so repressed that the man supposes it is dead. But one night he is alone in the desert under the starry sky; one day he stands with bowed head and damp eyes beside an open grave; or there comes an hour when he clings with desperate instinct to the wet rail of a storm-tossed boat, and suddenly out of the forgotten depths of his being this mysterious *something* leaps forth. It over-reaches habit; it pushes aside reason, and with a voice that will not be denied it cries out its questionings and its prayer.

"Now I lay me down to sleep!" What a prayer for a man like Scott, whose feet are fast in the stirrups, who hangs in double danger from the horns of a bull and the hoofs of his own horse, expecting within five seconds to be gored or trampled to death! Could any words be more ludicrous? Yet the form of the words is negligible. The significant fact, the amazing fact, is that such a man in such a situation prays, and the prayer he prays is the first he ever learned.

RELIGION ABOLISHED?

A physician of foreign birth, whose practise was on the lower East Side of New York, told me that almost everybody prays before he dies, and that no matter how long he has lived in America, or how well he may know the English language, he prays in the language to which he was born. Jesus of Nazareth on the Cross did so. Whether He could speak Greek we do not know; some of the men who stood near the Cross used that language and so could not understand Him when He cried: "Eloi, Eloi, lama sabachthani." But Mary, the mother, understood; it was their native Aramaic, the language of her little boy.

In one of his cleverest essays Maeterlinck considers the number of classifications and generalizations which a dog must make in early life, as, for instance, to decide whom he should admit through the door as a friend and at whom to dash out in the dark. He says that the dog does not spend much time in looking up at the sky; one glance is enough to show him that there is nothing he can dig out of that. But the earth may be dug into, and interesting objects found therein.

Man also digs in the earth and finds not only rabbits and woodchucks, but potatoes and oil and iron and gold. And he must dig or he can not live. But man has not been content, as has the dog, with a single upward glance. Delving away with aching arms, pushing himself relentlessly in the battle for existence, wherein all the forces of the universe seem to be his foes, he has continued to glance up. However absurdly, he has made himself believe that he is more than the beasts; that behind the riddle of the stars there is an answer; beyond the storm and sun, a Power, and that the Power can perhaps be bribed or persuaded to treat him as a friend. Uncontent to live and lust and die, he has fashioned himself religion.

How was it that he came to do this? Of what stuff is religion made? Has it been to man a help or a hindrance in his upward struggle? And whether a help or a hindrance, if it be merely the child of his own imagining, has he not now become strong enough to discard its assurance and walk courageously alone?

"If we go back to the beginning," Holbach wrote, "we shall find that ignorance and fear created the gods; that fancy, enthusiasm or deceit adorned or disfigured them; that weakness worships them; that credulity preserves them; and that custom respects and tyranny supports them in order to make the blindness of men serve its own interests."

RELIGION ABOLISHED?

This is one of those broad assertions which philosophic rebels like to utter but which, in poor theologians, they are quick to condemn. Whether fear and weakness created the gods no man can say, for no man now living was present when the gods were created, and all the records are long since gone. The German scholar, Heinrich Schmidt, assuming for the purpose of illustration that the first human beings were on this planet two hundred and fifty thousand years ago, tried to illustrate with a clock face the long period of unrecorded as against the brief period of recorded history. If the residence of the human race on earth be represented by the twelve hours from midnight to noon, and men began a few minutes after midnight to split bone in order to get the marrow out, or to chip flints for arrows, then they had a long time to work in the dark before they began to write down their progress. Measured on this clock face all recorded history, including the building of the Pyramids and much that went before, occurred in the last half-hour; and the events about which we have positive knowledge belong to the past five minutes.

We know that when the curtain of history is first lifted every race and tribe is revealed in possession of some sort of religion, but as to how or where primitive man began the first crude

creation of his faith the scientists can only conjecture. They imagine that his dreams may
have had something to do with it. Or perhaps
his shadow suggested another self, a kind of existence that was not solid and material. At least
he saw things happening about him when no one
was in sight to make them happen. The wind
blew; what made it blow? Water flowed from
under solid rock; what caused it to spring forth?
There was thunder and lighting and rain and
hail, and above all there was the sun. What
made the thunder, the lightning, the rain, the
dark and the life-giving sun?

Primitive man wondered, and gradually he
began to make the great discovery of personality.
He himself did the things he wanted done, and he
supposed that the objects about him were also
alive and did as they chose. He assumed that a
spirit lived in the spring, and a god rode in the
storm, and that the sun was the greatest of all the
gods. As for the wind, the very word "spirit"
means just that. So, in the beginning, there
were presumably as many gods as there were
things to be explained, both good and bad.
There must have been a god for the east wind
and for the west wind, a god for the sunshine and
a god for the rain, a god not only for joy and
pain but for each of the many joys and pains,
the good luck and the sorrows.

Primitive man made another discovery: he found out that he could do things without being where the things he did were done. That is, he could throw a stone and knock over a rabbit twenty yards away. He could shoot an arrow and kill a deer. Presumably his gods also could hurl stones or thunder-bolts and shoot arrows and accomplish results at a distance. His gods were never very far away; the heavens in those days were not high, but he was conscious of them, and the crude beginnings of gratitude were born in him when the gods seemed to be on his side. Coming through the long desert and finding suddenly a cool spring, he thanked his gods for the refreshment; feeling the cold raw blasts give way before the conquering power of the sun, he humbled himself and prayed. He began to have some better qualities, that primitive beast-like man.

But he had his terrible side as well. He butchered his enemy without mercy and drank the blood. He lived long before Harvey's discovery of the circulation, but when he slit a throat the blood spurted, and to him that spurting was a manifestation of life in the blood. He came to believe that blood was precious, sacred. It was his habit to divide with his gods whatever good things he gained; he thought the gods liked

21

the flavor and smoke of cooking meat and that above all they liked blood. So bloody sacrifice entered into religions.

Thus we have our imaginary picture of primitive man in his two aspects: the beginnings in him of gratitude and affection, and the equally strong beginnings of cruelty, of superstition born of fear. But somehow in the process of his development a strange thing occurred. There entered into that rude heart from somewhere a consciousness of what we call sin. He had committed some evil act and got away with it unrebuked—some particularly atrocious murder, some more than usually violent rape, some triumph within him of brute passion where his feeble reason taught him better—and this act left him not happy but depressed. This was an extraordinary experience, for not in all the history of the brute creation had it occurred before.

The Book of Genesis records it allegorically with the story of Adam and Eve and the forbidden fruit. What the real experience was, or whether there was any one experience or only a slow accretion of many, we may leave to the philosophers and theologians to inquire. But the fact is unmistakable. In some great hour for the human race, primitive man felt struggling

22

through his hatred and his lust a faint protest from a dawning conscience; he was ashamed, and trembled and hid himself from the gods. That experience in the old theology has been labeled the "fall of man," but if it was a fall it was a fall forward. The man had become like God, knowing good and evil. It was the first great upward step.

The first blood sacrifices, as we have conjectured, may have been a generous desire to share with the gods. Men liked meat, and the gods were nourished by the fragrant odor of it and the gratitude of the worshiper. But with the dawning of the sense of sin sacrifice took on a different aspect. Sacrifice was for sin and a means of forgiveness. It took a good while to work out the theory concretely, but little by little the generosity of the free-will offering became merged in the semi-penal form of sin-offering. And there was more and more occasion for blood, which had, let us admit, a certain harsh educational value. Men learned, however cruelly, that sin was expensive and destructive; it cost life.

Obviously, however, this system of sacrifices for sin had one sad result. It became a means of placating or bribing the gods. Sin was not always a breach of the moral law; it was any-

thing which people imagined that the gods did
not like, and the gods were by no means always
moral, nor were the deeds at which they took
offense invariably those that made men undesir-
able neighbors. Whatever displeased the gods,
whether grave or trivial, must be paid for in
blood, and if not the blood of the man who had
sinned then the blood of some one else. The
blood of an enemy would sometimes answer the
requirement, but for the most costly offense it
must be the blood of a friend. The more
precious the person the more the gods rejoiced
in the blood. Thus many ancient peoples, including even some of those who are told about
in the Bible, sacrificed their own children.

It is a tenacious thing, this idea of bloody
sacrifice; it still hangs on. Religion to many
people is even now something that hurts, and
God is an unhappy being who will not be appeased or bribed to good conduct except through
self-abasement and pain.

So much for conjecture. In some such
fashion as we have described scientists imagine
that faith had its birth in the human heart. Man,
who fought the earth and its beasts for a living,
who shook with terror in the storm, and died
from exposure or the blows of his fellows, had
the effrontery to conceive that his life was im-

portant in the eyes of Beings beyond the stars, that whether he did his best or not was a matter of some consequence in this world and, perhaps, even in a world to come. Very much later, many thousand years later, when the race began to make written records, a more dramatic history of the beginnings of religion was evolved, such a story as we have in the opening books of the Old Testament. Moses believed that the Ten Commandments which he brought down from the mountain for the children of Israel were handed to him direct from God. We know that he had learned most of them as a lad in Egypt, where the number of the commandments was not ten but forty-two, each with a special god to look after it. The Code of Hammurabi, seven or eight hundred years before Moses, has the same injunctions against lying, theft and murder, and the stone tablet on which the two hundred and eighty-two laws of Hammurabi are inscribed bears a picture of the great law-giver receiving them from his god.

Did Hammurabi lie? Did Moses lie? Not a bit. Both believed, as had every prophet, that the message he uttered was no mere invention of his own. And they were right. Whatever share each one had in the wording and recording of the law and its arrangement and application,

25

no one of these men made it up. These great underlying truths are older than any of the men whose names have attached to them; they are the cumulative conscience of the race, and had their beginnings on the day when the first man sinned and trembled, and did not know why.

"Just a minute," somebody exclaims. "Let us get you straight on this. Do you believe that God created conscience in men and has slowly but steadily, through the ages, enlightened it? Or do you believe that men's conscience created the idea of God and has slowly, through the ages, recreated Him in more worthy image, as conscience has developed and knowledge grown?"

If the gentleman who raises this question will continue with us through this book, he will discover later an attempt at an answer. Meanwhile, let us assume for the purposes of this chapter that it makes no difference.

If you believe that there is a God who created men and women, starting them off as naked, clawless and hornless beings, compelled to fight for existence against the lion, the bear and the rattlesnake, then the God of such beings had to be content with very meager beginnings in the matter of religion. And it was no more debasing to His nature to be worshiped by crude and even cruel rites than it is debasing to Him to put a drop of His being into the bulb sunk into the slime that is later to blossom as a water-lily. He was working with very rough material in those first days, working on a long-time program which could not go too fast.

If, on the other hand, you believe that men fashioned gods in their own image and, as their minds and hearts improved, have made their gods constantly better, you are also welcome, in this chapter, to hold to that view.

Historically, the result is the same. Religion has moved forward from lower to higher planes. The prophets of each succeeding epoch have uttered the moral requirements in nobler language, proclaiming always that what they uttered was the voice of God. The Jehovah of Joshua who commanded the Israelites to slay their enemies, sparing none, not even the women and children, was in moral grandeur far below the level of the Jehovah of Jonah who refused to destroy the city of Nineveh "wherein are more than sixscore thousand persons that cannot discern between their right hand and their left hand; and also much cattle." And Jonah's God, in turn, rises to no such height as the Father of Jesus who could "so love the world that He gave His only begotten Son."

Step by step through the ages religion has

grown finer in its conception of God and its statement of the moral law. Even the most critical of skeptics will hardly deny that, with all its wickedness and cruelties, it has been a lifting force, a ladder for the upward climb. But the toughest part of the climb is over. We have achieved civilization, and it looks reasonably secure. We are full-grown men at last and need no myths; let us face the facts.

The facts in the case *against* religion are threefold.

In the first place, science has banished many of the mysteries that were so long inscrutable. We know that the thunder is not God's voice, nor the lightning the agency of His wrath, for Franklin captured the lightning with a string attached to a kite and bottled it, and we have learned to make it jump to light our homes at the touch of a button, or travel the tread-mill of a motor to do our family washing.

I stood one day on the top of a little adobe hut, looking down into the courtyard where the Hopi Indians were carrying on the solemn ritual of their snake dance, probably the oldest religious ceremony on this continent and one that has never yet been tainted with commercialism. Four thousand people, Indians and whites, made up the colorful audience that had driven miles across the open desert to wait all afternoon in the hot sun. In stately rhythm the men of the Snake Tribe danced around the stone that is supposed to cover the opening to the lower regions, carrying their rattlesnakes clutched in their teeth. And when the ceremony was finished the boys of the tribe gathered the snakes into their hands and ran swiftly to the four corners of the compass to release them in order that they might scatter across the desert and bring back the rain.

It was all very impressive, and even the most cynical tourist who had made the journey in his high powered car was silent and a little serious. But most impressive of all to me were not the Indian men with their venomous reptiles, but the squaws who, having seen the dance many times, did not press forward into the crowd but stood with their naked papooses on the tops of the houses farther back. Their eyes were turned away from the ceremony, in the other direction. Silently they searched the heavens for the sign of a cloud which would promise rain. Faithfully, wordlessly, they waited, as how many millions of women have waited through the ages, to know whether their men would succeed in persuading the gods to be good.

It is said that the Hopi snake dance has

never failed to bring the rains, and on the front page of the *Kansas City Star* I read, as the train carried me East, that there had been a deluge on the Hopi reservation on the day following the dance which I, myself, had seen. The report was doubtless true. If it was we know, or at least we think we know, that the dance had nothing to do with it; that "atmospheric conditions" responding to "natural laws" brought the rain in their own good time. This much our science has told us, and we look at the Hopis with a curious interest and are thankful that the rain held off until we got back to Flagstaff. For our freedom from such "superstition" we are complacently grateful. Science furnishes no evidence that God interrupts the reign of natural laws in response to human petition.

On the contrary, there is disconcerting evidence that natural laws have neither respect for human rights nor any sense of moral values. Sir Richard Burton, who made the famous tours into Arabian lands and gave us so rich a body of Oriental literature, visited a tribe who inquired eagerly if he knew where Allah could be found.

"Why do you want to know?" he asked.

"If we could find him we would spear him on the spot," they answered. "It is he who has been burning up our pastures, and giving us no rain, and killing our cattle and our wives."

Similarly, the great thinker John Stuart Mill exclaimed: "In sober truth all the things which men are imprisoned or hanged for doing to each other are nature's every day performance."

The earthquake at Lisbon in 1755 shook the faith of even the most devout thinkers of that time. Here were thirty thousand people, crowded into their churches on All Saints' Day, making their humble supplications to a supposedly loving God, when suddenly, and without warning, the churches were hurled down upon their helpless heads, burying them in the ruins. Voltaire, learning that the French clergy were explaining the disaster as a punishment for the sins of the people of Lisbon, could not withhold his wrath and broke out with devastating lines:

"I am a puny part of the great whole.
Yes; but all animals condemned to live,
All sentient things, born by the same stern law,
Suffer like me, and like me also die.
The vulture fastens on his timid prey,
And stabs with bloody beak the quivering limbs:
All's well, it seems, for it. But in a while
An eagle tears the vulture into shreds;
The eagle is transfixed by shafts of man;
The man, prone in the dust of battlefields,
Mingling his blood with dying fellow men,

Becomes in turn the food of ravenous birds.
Thus the whole world in every member groans,
All born for torment and for mutual death.
And o'er this ghastly chaos you would say
The ills of each make up the good of all!
What blessedness! And as, with quaking voice,
Mortal and pitiful ye cry, 'All's well,'
The universe belies you, and your heart
Refutes a hundred times your mind's con-
    ceit. . . .
What is the verdict of the vastest mind?
Silence: the book of fate is closed to us.
Man is a stranger to his own research;
He knows not whence he comes, nor whither
    goes.
Tormented atoms in a bed of mud,
Devoured by death, a mockery of fate;
But thinking atoms, whose far-seeing eyes,
Guided by thoughts, have measured the faint
    stars.
Our being mingles with the infinite;
Ourselves we never see or come to know."

    Voltaire was no "atheist" as the narrow
clerics of his day proclaimed. The charge of
atheism has been the too ready cry of formalism
against all courageous thinkers; even Socrates
was denounced by pious Athenians as "the
atheist who says there is only one God." Voltaire
erected a church to God and has left us a clear
and noble statement of his faith. But hundreds

of thousands of the men and women of his day were atheists, and some of them were made so by that Lisbon earthquake. They could no longer tolerate a deity who would slaughter thirty thousand people gathered humbly in his worship. So in that age, and in all ages, the wickedness of nature has grasped hands with the widening discoveries of science as the second great fact in the case against religion.

The third fact in the case is man's growing independence. While the struggle for existence still hung in the balance, man needed the help of whatever gods there were. But the struggle is nearly, if not entirely, won. Famine has been banished from all well organized communities. Modern nations have solved their problems of production; when farmers are in trouble these days it is not usually because they have raised too little but because they have raised too much. It has been remarked by many historians that so long as men live in the country and get their sustenance direct from the soil they tend to be religious. They are inescapably conscious of their dependence upon the favor of the elements. But transport them into cities and that consciousness diminishes. There, life is ordered by powers that can be felt and seen and measurably controlled. Food comes from the grocery, and water from the tap; neither the sun nor the clouds are facts of supreme importance.

Similarly, prosperity has almost always been accompanied by a decline of religion. Even so faithful a believer as Sir Francis Bacon noted that fact, saying: "The causes of atheism are, divisions in religion, if they be many; for any one division addeth zeal to both sides; but many divisions introduce atheism. . . . And lastly, learned times, especially with peace and prosperity, for troubles and adversities do more bow men's minds to religion."

To which we may properly add the testimony of Seelye, the great teacher and divine: "Religious feeling is generally strong in proportion to the sense of weakness and helplessness. It is when man's own resources fail that he looks most anxiously to find a friend in the universe. Religion is man's consolation in the presence of a necessity which he cannot resist; his refuge when he is deserted by his own power of energy or ingenuity. Negroes are religious; the primitive races, in the presence of natural phenomena which they could not calculate or resist, were intensely religious; women in their dependence are more religious than men; Orientals under despotic governments are more religious than the nations of the West. On the other hand, a time of great advance in power, whether scientific power over nature, or the power to avert evils, given by wealth and prosperity, is commonly a time of decline in religious feeling."

In other words, the ladder of faith is good while you are down and struggling to get up, but it is normally forgotten when you have arrived. We are in the sort of age which Seelye describes in his last sentence. The "advance in power over nature" has been greater than ever before. "Wealth and prosperity" have increased beyond all dreams, and so skilfully are we beginning to master the intricacies of the "business cycle" that there are some, including Henry Ford, who believe that "a hundred years of prosperity" lie ahead. If that be true the outlook for religion, according to the observations of Bacon and Seelye, is not bright. Science goes on merrily stripping the universe of the mysteries which once were religion's stock in trade. Nature continues unmoral regardless of all preaching of the rule of a loving God. And prosperity is becoming so abundant as to conquer the sense of need.

Does not all this mean that the days of religion are past? Should we now abolish without regret what we have seemingly outgrown? Is it time to welcome bravely the new day of science, of natural law, of prosperity humanly created and controlled?

Before we give a final answer, and just as a matter of historic interest, we may pause long enough on the threshold of this glorious era to reflect that it is not without precedent. On several occasions in the past humanity has seemingly won its upward struggle and been blessed with power and plenty. There came such a period in the latter days of Greece.

A marvelous company of human intellects gave splendor to that period. The single little city of Athens boasted more men of first-class genius than the whole world managed to produce in several centuries afterward. Pericles ruled with vision and tolerance. He had no taste for war. Instead he sought the welfare of all citizens and erected as monuments those works of art, including the Parthenon, that have been the envy and despair of all builders. Euripides and Aristophanes and Æschylus produced plays that are still studied as models. Phidias and a shining group of sculptors lifted art to perfection. Socrates began to teach the processes of inquiry by which the human mind has won its subsequent victories, and one of his disciples, Plato, dared to dream and to write of a perfect commonwealth. It was indeed a golden age.

RELIGION ABOLISHED?

To the north of Greece there came a little later a monarch, Philip of Macedonia, who dreamed of an empire that should spread over all the east, carrying Greek culture everywhere. He knew that his dream was too big for a single lifetime and so he sought to educate his son, Alexander, more carefully than any prince had been trained before. He employed the best minds of the age as teachers, heading them up with Aristotle, the pupil of Plato, the man whose mind ruled the intellectual world for many centuries.

The mother of the prince was even more ambitious, so much so that she poisoned the boy's mind against his father. Thus when news of Philip's victories came back to court, Alexander, instead of rejoicing as a natural son might be expected to do, was outspokenly jealous.

"Father will get everything in advance, boys," he complained to his companions. "He won't leave any great task for me to share with you."

The mother was a weird neurotic sort of woman, a devotee of dark religious rites in which snakes, and sexual orgies, and revolting sacrifices all played a part. She quarreled with Philip and left the court, taking Alexander with her. Later, when Philip was stabbed to death, she openly rejoiced and insisted that funeral honors equal to those given to the king should be paid to the murderers. She was no good influence for her son when he returned in triumph to take charge of the great empire which his father's genius had created.

Alexander started brilliantly, though with cruel excess. He consolidated his father's conquests in Greece, burning the rebellious cities and levying on their populations for larger armies. He crossed to Asia Minor and captured Sidon and Tyre, razing the latter to the ground. He conquered the whole decadent empire of Darius; he invaded Egypt and founded at the mouth of the Nile the new city of Alexandria, which for a century afterward was the intellectual capital of the world. Here, under his successor Ptolomy, science made its first brilliant conquests. Here Euclid wrote the works on mathematics that still are used in our schools; here Archimedes came to study—the man who said: "Give me a lever long enough and strong enough, and a place to stand on, and I will move the world"; here Herophilus made researches into human anatomy, dissecting the bodies of condemned criminals while they were still alive.

These men came after Alexander had gone, but they worked in the city that he built and

were supported by a monarch who had been one
of his generals; let us give credit where credit is
due.

As for Alexander himself, his genius was
much too restless for scientific research or solid
building. He must be on his way, seeking another king to subdue, a new nation to add to
his empire, as if there were always the hope that
the next victory might bring satisfaction, that
beyond the next range of mountains he should
find the answer to the great *why* of life. He
marched through the Libyan desert in order to
consult the oracle of Jupiter Ammon, whose
priest saluted him as a son of Jove. Perhaps
thereafter he began to believe that he really was
a son of Jove, at least he acted as though he did,
and he was very angry with his companions when
they ridiculed his pretensions. He finished the
conquest of Egypt; he humbled all of India that
could be reached. Nowhere in the world was
there any organized power to give him the
stimulus of a good fight. He had whipped it
all; he was the supreme master; he was not yet
thirty, and there was no more.

His search for contentment was tragic. He
married Oriental princesses. He drank. To
gratify the whim of Thais, an Athenian
courtesan, he set fire to Persepolis, the wonder

of the ancient world, and reduced it to an ash heap. When Hephæstion, his favorite, died he determined on a display of grief such as the world had never known. He pulled down the battlements of neighboring cities, and slew by thousands the unhappy inhabitants of captured towns; he levied a ransom of millions upon the country for a gilded tomb.

These things did Alexander when he had conquered the world. But in the doing of them there was no inner peace, no satisfaction. "There are no more worlds to conquer," he exclaimed, and, weeping, he threw himself into a drunken debauch. Being tired of living, he died.

Let us glance at another prosperous period and another king. He identifies himself as the "son of David, king in Jerusalem," and his book describes his efforts to find happiness and contentment in life. He began by studying all the books and seeking wisdom from every source. He thought this would give him peace, but he found that when he had "gotten more wisdom than all they that have been in Jerusalem" he was less happy than before.

"For in much wisdom is much grief: and he that increaseth knowledge increaseth sorrow."

He set forth then on another tack. He

would seek pleasure; life was a joke without meaning. All right, let us laugh and forget.

"I said in mine heart, Go to now, I will prove thee with mirth, therefore, enjoy pleasure. . . .

"I sought in mine heart to give myself unto wine, yet acquainting mine heart with wisdom; and to lay hold on folly, till I might see what was that good for the sons of men, which they should do under the heaven all the days of their life."

But there was no comfort at the end of this path either. So he threw himself into industry. He did great works; he built houses; he planted vineyards; he had servants and many possessions.

"I gathered me also silver and gold, and the peculiar treasure of kings and of the provinces: I gat me men singers and women singers, and the delights of the sons of men, as musical instruments, and that of all sorts.

"So I was great, and increased more than all that were before me in Jerusalem: also my wisdom remained with me.

"And whatsoever mine eyes desired I kept not from them, I withheld not my heart from any joy."

Like Alexander he had youth, wealth, fame, health, physical and mental delights. But, says he:

WHAT CAN A MAN BELIEVE?

"I looked on all the works that my hands had wrought, and on the labour that I had laboured to do: and, behold, all was vanity, and vexation of spirit, and there was no profit under the sun."

A discouraging confession from one who had all the things that the rest of us are trying so hard to obtain. Is this what waits at the top of the ladder? Is this to be the last chapter in human life when every want is satisfied: tears and drunkenness because there are no more worlds to conquer; vanity of vanities, vexation of the spirit?

"A time of great advance in power, of . . . wealth and prosperity," said Seelye, "is commonly a time of decline in religious feeling."

We are on the threshold of such a time, a period when more people will have larger prosperity than ever before. It is conceivable, even, that all of us might get everything we want.

As Alexander did . . . and this other, older king.

CHAPTER II

LET us present the facts against the church in the strongest possible terms. History furnishes plenty of material.

The scene is the desert, the home of camels and sheiks, of green oases and brown veiled women; the birthplace of more than one religion. The Korashites and the Ghatafananti have joined in an expedition to finish off Mohammed. On their way to Medina, where the prophet is entrenched behind a ditch and moat (novelties in desert warfare), they induce a Jewish tribe, the Beni Koraida, to enlist.

The prophet of Allah has enemies inside the ditch as well as out; the Jews of Medina are related to the Beni Koraida and are likely to attack him in the rear. Panic-stricken, he suggests to his captains that they bribe the Ghatafananti to separate peace by offering them a third of the date harvest of Medina. The suggestion is hardly made before a chief of tremendous

43

fatness struggles to his feet. It is Sa'd b. Mu'adh, leader of the Awsites.

"Do you propose this by the command of Allah, or is it an idea of your own?" he demands.

The prophet is never off his guard.

"If it had been a command of Allah I should never have asked your advice," he replies. "I see you pressed by your enemies on every side, and I seek to break their confederacy."

"O prophet of God!" rejoins Sa'd, "when we were fellow-idolaters with these people of Ghatafan they got none of our dates without paying for them; and shall we give them up gratuitously now that we are of the true faith and led by thee? No, by Allah! if they want our dates they must win them by their swords!"

Heartened by this stout speech, the followers of the prophet prepare to stand firm, while he himself sends spies to sow dissension in the ranks of his enemies, a form of diplomacy at which he excels. So successful is the effort that the allied tribes are shortly quarreling vigorously and when, a day or two later, a storm comes to blow down their tents, put out their fires and drench them to the skin, a rumor spreads that Moham- med has raised the storm by enchantment. This is too much. Grumbling and cursing, the foes break their camp and hurry back to their homes.

MORE HARM THAN GOOD?

Within the walls of Medina is great rejoicing. The prophet is tempted to be satisfied with his victory, but the angel of Allah upbraids him. He must not rest until vengeance has been visited upon the Beni Koraida. So the faithful surround this Jewish tribe in its fortified city and presently compel a surrender. The Beni Koraida implore the intercession of their ancient friends the Awsites, and the prophet agrees to leave their fate to the decision of the chief of the Awsites, our fat friend Sa'd. Joyously the Beni Koraida come forth, sure that the judgment will be merciful. But Sa'd is hot and sweaty and suffering from a spear thrust in his side.

"Will ye then," he inquires of his tribesmen, "bind yourselves by the covenant of God that whatsoever I decide ye will accept?"

They agree.

"Then this is my judgment," he shouts. "The men shall be put to death, the women and children sold into slavery, and the spoils divided among the faithful."

A torrent of protest is silenced by the prophet.

"Truly the judgment of Sa'd is the judgment of God," he cries.

That night trenches are dug, and the next morning six or seven hundred men march out, seat themselves on the edge, and are beheaded and tumbled, one after another, into the long deep grave. The victors look on with gibes and sneers, the Prophet of God in the front rank. After a time he tires of the spectacle and goes back to his harem which the expedition has enriched by a beautiful young Jewess. A few days later he emerges to pronounce a final benediction over the body of the fat Saad whose wound, reopened in the excitement of his judgment, bled him to death.

"O Lord, verily Sa'd hath labored in thy service," the prophet prays. "He hath believed in thy Prophet, and hath fulfilled his covenant. Wherefore do thou, O Lord, receive his spirit with the best reception wherewith thou receivest a departing soul!"

Undoubtedly, the priests of the Beni Koraida, waiting at the edge of the ditch for the sword to reach them, had uttered similar prayers. Their souls were wafted up to Heaven only a few days before the soul of Sa'd.

We now step forward nine hundred years. The scene is Rome, not in the days of the Cæsars but at the time when the church is supreme. It is a day of solemn thanksgiving and devout religious worship in the comparatively recent year of our Lord, 1572. By special order of the

Pope, Gregory XIII, a *Te Deum* is being sung.
What inspiring event calls forth this historic
hymn of praise?

Nothing less than the murder of twenty thousand Christians by brutal butchery.

For centuries fighting had gone on between
the Catholics and Protestants of France, with
shameful cruelties on both sides. As far back
as 1208, Simon de Montfort had organized a
group of knights who pledged themselves to
subdue their heretical fellow countrymen. All
peaceful attempts having failed to persuade the
wanderers to return to the one true fold, Simon
took the city of Beziers and proceeded to
slaughter all of its fifteen thousand inhabitants
regardless of age, sex or creed.

"How shall we know the heretics from the
faithful?" he had previously inquired of Milon,
the Papal Legate, who had been sent by Inno-
cent III to preach the crusade.

To which the personal representative of the
Holy Father had answered: "Kill them all. God
will be able to recognize His own."

This, as we have said, was in 1208. Three
hundred years had passed, and the wiser heads
in France realized that the incessant warfare
was impoverishing the country. At the feast of
St. Germain in 1570 a peace was consummated

in token of which the king's sister was to be given in marriage to Henry of Navarre. Leaders of both parties were invited to Paris in celebration of the nuptials. The city was filled with Protestants, long shut out but now rejoicing in the new era of peace and tolerance. It was too good an opportunity to be lost, so thought Catherine de Medici, the Queen Mother, and her fanatical advisers. A little ruthlessness now and the offending heretics would be stamped out altogether.

The matter was planned with care. The bells rang forth at midnight—the signal being given by Catherine herself—and before morning the streets were red with the blood of twenty thousand Christians, slaughtered for the glory of Christ.

This was the massacre of St. Bartholomew's Day. This was the news that was carried to Rome and, by special order of Gregory XIII, caused the *Te Deum* to ascend to Heaven. If souls have ears one wonders if Mohammed and our fat friend Sa'd enjoyed that noble anthem.

At this point in our story many Catholics, and perhaps some Mohammedans, will take their pens in hand to send us harsh words of protest. We ask them to forbear. Bigotry and cruelty have not been a monopoly of any sect, or sects.

All have helped to make the records terrible.

Another picture.

Nineteen years before the massacre of St. Bartholomew's Day the city of Geneva was ruled by John Calvin. He had rebelled against the Roman Catholic Church and gone forth to establish a reformed faith. So powerful was he in personality, as well as in doctrine, that he held the government of the city in his hands. Laws were administered according to his will, and religious regularity was the test of civic rights. His rule was not without opposition, to be sure. The old Genevan families resented the dominance of this foreigner who, having fled to the city for protection, proceeded to take it over and handle it according to his own inflexible ideas of the will of God. The opposition grew steadily between 1548 and 1553, when a fortunate event occurred to turn the scale in Calvin's favor. That event was the arrest in Geneva of Dr. Miguel Servetus.

A brilliant young fellow, Servetus—a Spaniard who had studied medicine and is credited with having been the first to discover the pulmonary circulation of the blood. He settled in Vienne in France, where he built up a profitable practise. If only he had been content to stick to his scalpels and his pills he would have grown rich, lived long and died forgotten. But there was a restless spirit of inquiry within him. He stirred around among the churchly creeds and found items which seemed to him mistaken. He published a book, *De Trinitstis Erroribus,* regarding erroneous ideas of the Trinity. A layman at this distance finds it difficult to understand just what he was driving at, or why anybody should have been particularly concerned. But the righteous were deeply stirred, and none more so than John Calvin with whom Dr. Servetus had engaged in uncomplimentary correspondence before, criticizing one of Calvin's books. Servetus was promptly arrested and condemned in Vienne; he escaped from jail and, for some strange reason which no one exactly comprehends, made his way to Geneva.

At once he was arrested. His enemies sought to delay the case and save the victim, but they only made trouble for themselves. Servetus had shocked the prejudices of orthodox Europe. Calvin, in forcing his sentence, was backed up by an almost universal public opinion. When the poor doctor was led out to the stake, and the fire was lighted under him, the smoke of his burning carried away most of the opposition to John Calvin. Servetus had come at a lucky hour. Heresy was stamped out in the holy town of Geneva; the foes of the Lord's appointed were put to rout; Calvin was reestablished firmly in his seat of power, and the cost of it all was only one heretic burned—a mischievous fellow who had foolishly tried to think about God in his own independent fashion.

Step over now to Germany.

When the peasants revolted against their intolerable lot they might naturally have expected to find a sympathetic friend in that arch-revolter, Martin Luther. Surely his heart, which beat so fiercely against the evils of Rome, would have a tender spot for those who sought to rectify their economic evils. Not at all.

"A rebel is outlawed of God and Kaiser," said this prophet contemptuously. "Therefore who can and will first slaughter such a man, does right well, since upon such a common rebel every man is alike judge and executioner. Therefore who can shall here openly or secretly smite, slaughter and stab; and hold that there is nothing more poisonous, more harmful, more devilish than a rebellious man."

Not very pleasant words to come from the follower of One who had said: "Come unto me all ye that labor and are heavy laden, and I will give you rest." The masters of those that "labored and were heavy laden" in Luther's day racked them and flayed them and tore out their tongues with red-hot pincers. Of two of them who were being burned the chronicles report: "They lived long and cried with all their hearts to God; it was pitiable to hear them."

But no word of pity or comfort came from Martin Luther. They were outside the pale. They had dared to attempt a different position in society, which was a crime second only to the greatest crime of all—daring to believe differently about their God.

We pass by England. The stories of hangings and burnings and plunderings there are familiar enough to us all. Let us stop for a moment on our own fair shores, land of the free and home of the brave. Here surely we shall find no record of cruelties for righteousness' sake; this continent, settled by those who had fled from religious persecution abroad, must always have held out a tolerant welcome to worshipers of any faith. Let us see.

In the days when everybody in Boston was a good church-member, and the preachers ruled the town almost as thoroughly as John Calvin had ruled Geneva, there was an active-minded lady named Anne Hutchinson, a devout worshiper in the congregation of Rev. John Cotton. It was her partiality for Dr. Cotton's preaching which had caused her to leave her comfortable home in England for our wilderness shores, and this same enthusiasm was the beginning of her troubles.

So eager was she to extract the last drop of benefit from the Sunday morning discourse that she formed a group of women who met weekly in her home and listened to her own repetition of it. The times were dreary. There was no entertainment for faithful wives in the dour town of Boston. Surely this weekly gathering, the first woman's club in the land, would seem to have been praiseworthy and free from any blame.

But not so. As her meetings increased in popularity Mistress Anne grew bolder, embroidering the pure doctrine of the preacher with some ideas of her own. Pious ideas. Amazingly harmless ideas, as seen from this distance. But the field of ideas was reserved for the clergy, and none must trespass on it. Only a little time passed before Mistress Anne was brought up short, "convented," as the record has it, "for traducing the ministers and their ministry in this country."

One of the charges against her was so heinous that even her adored pastor left her side and joined himself to her accusers. She had dared to express a doubt as to whether the same body which is consigned to the grave would rise, unchanged, at the resurrection. Such heresy was intolerable. If there was doubt as to the identity of bodies in the resurrection, what horrid complications would not arise!

Said her pastor solemnly: "You can not then evade the argument pressed on you by our brother Buckle and others, that filthy sin of community women, and all other promiscuous coming together of men and women without distinction or relation of marriage. . . . Though I have not heard, neither do I think, you have been unfaithful to your husband in his marriage covenant," he added grudgingly, "yet that will follow upon it."

The sentence which was pronounced on Mrs. Hutchinson has come down to us.

"In the name of the Lord Jesus Christ, and the name of the church, I do not only pronounce you worthy to be cast out, but I do cast you out! and in the name of Christ I do deliver you up to Satan that you may learn no more to blaspheme, and to seduce and to lie; And I do account you from this time forth to be a Heathen and a Publican, and so to be held of all the Brethren and Sisters of this congregation and of others; therefore I command you in the name of Jesus Christ and of His church, as a leper to withdraw yourself out of this congregation."

MORE HARM THAN GOOD?

The climate was bleak. The woods were full of Indians and wild animals. Mrs. Hutchinson was pregnant. She went forth from the town and with her went that splendid little rebel who insisted on making every fight her own, Mary Dyer, also pregnant. Both women promptly miscarried, which was interpreted by the pious as an evidence of their guilt.

Anne Hutchinson's sentence might have been even more severe but she was strongly connected in the colony. No such connections operated to spare Mary Dyer, who for twenty years was a thorn in the flesh of the authorities. The colony having enacted horrible laws against the Quakers, Mary determined to test them, having as helpers two Englishmen, William Robinson and Marmaduke Stevenson. The three were condemned to death, and the men were hanged on Boston Common before Mary's eyes. She herself climbed the ladder to the scaffold, the halter was put around her neck, and her eyes covered with a handkerchief furnished by the Rev. Mr. Wilson who had jeered at her two predecessors. At that moment a messenger burst theatrically through the crowd with the cry: "Stop, for she is reprieved."

It was the intention to scare her so thoroughly that she would refrain from agitation in the future, but Mary was not that kind. After a few months of recuperation she was busy again, and this time there was no reprieve. The same "Priest Wilson" was on hand to make her last moments more unhappy. She never flinched. Pert and unrepentant to the last, she was hung up "as a flag for others to take example by," as one of her judges cynically expressed it. Hung up on Boston Common by those who, having fought for the right to worship God according to their own fashion, were unwilling that any should worship Him otherwise.

"It is the Shame and Reproach of New England," said William Coddington, once treasurer of the Massachusetts Colony and later governor of Rhode Island, "that those that were persecuted in England and bore their testimonies against Bishops and Ceremonies should in New England put to death four of the servants of the ever living God, banish upon pain of death, cut off ears, fine, whip and imprison, for keeping their consciences pure to God. . . ." But he adds: "The Magistrates were priest ridden . . . they (the preachers) would have Accommodations for Lands, and the Best Houses built for them; now were they grown warm in their Accommodations; now was the iron bed, like that of the Tyrant made use of, to cut all according to it shorter or longer. . . ."

MORE HARM THAN GOOD?

At The Hague is a museum filled with instruments of torture that freeze your blood. If all hell were to sit up for a night devising ways in which to wring the utmost possible pain from human flesh, it is difficult to imagine that anything could be added. Every organ of the body, and of the bodies of both sexes, has received its due measure of attention. There is nothing left for cruelty to devise. You turn your eyes away in horror, and then the thought flashes into your mind: "These are the fruits of faith. All these playthings of the fiends were invented amid prayer and fasting. Invented that Christians might correct one another regarding doctrines of which Jesus of Nazareth never heard."

If the crimes against men's bodies have been horrible, the outrage of their minds by the church has been even more costly. Persecution destroyed its thousands or ten thousands, but ignorance kept the whole world dark for centuries. And the church was the friend and protector of ignorance. Strange that it should have been so. Extraordinary that a faith which begins with the words "let there be light," whose great Prophet said: "I came that ye might have life, and that ye might have it more abundantly"—that such a church should have stood like rock against every effort of the human mind

57

to live more fully. By what weird perversion did this come to pass? What were the beginnings of the "conflict between science and theology" that darkened the lives of so many fine men and held the world back for centuries?

In the beginnings of the race there was neither science nor priesthood. No division of labor had taken place. Every man was his own blacksmith, tailor, arrow-maker, physician and priest. Tribes integrated for protection. When it was discovered one day that a particular member of the tribe was more skilful than the others in chipping flint, somebody conceived the idea that the whole tribe would fight more effectively if this one member were left behind to make arrows, his product being more accurate and deadly. So he was relieved from fighting but, having contributed his skill, he still shared equally in the spoils.

From such rude beginnings came the slow emergence of the crafts. The smith, forger of swords and plow-shares, was a mighty man in all tribes, and his descendants still dominate the telephone directory. The butcher, baker and candle-stick maker, all stepped out after thousands of years and with them, or after them—it is all conjecture, of course—came a man who was recognized as a specialist in the spiritual and esthetic sphere. Perhaps he was a singing dervish and worker of enchantments, who looked wisely at the stars or the entrails of a bird and foretold the future. Probably in his beginnings he was even more primitive. But he emerged along with the craftsmen, and from the earliest days of recorded history in Egypt we find him in the dual capacity of priest and physician, the custodian of both science and religion. Between them in those days there was no conflict. They were one.

This condition of peace and amity continued for perhaps five thousand years. But about the sixth century B. C. things began to shape themselves for a change. Thales of Miletus, who lived from 640 to 546 B. C., went down to Egypt and brought back the rudiments of astronomy and mathematics. He found them in the Egyptian temples, comfortably established as part of the religion; but as Greece was already well supplied with religions he left the Egyptian faith behind and took only the Egyptian sciences. It was the first rift. A little later, in Ionia, and apparently as a result of his influence, it began to be taught that the universe was governed by fixed laws. That was a new and revolutionary thought—the idea that men might find out important facts through observation, and not merely through the cultivation of the gods. From that time forward the story began to be a sad one. The priests felt their precincts encroached upon. Proudly and angrily they maintained their claim to intellectual monopoly. Their stubborn resistance delayed the process of enlightenment but could not prevent it. Slowly, bit by bit, men learned, and inevitably some of the things they learned contradicted directly the things which the priests had divined. The long battle was on.

A very able and very righteous man was in large measure responsible for crystallizing the conflict. He lived a thousand years afterward, and the church still holds him in high respect under the title of St. Augustine. Much that he wrote was fine and tolerant and inspiring, and his life was a sincere attempt to conform to the teachings of Jesus, as he interpreted them. Yet in one single sentence he probably did as much damage as any man has ever done with a stroke of the pen.

"Nothing is to be accepted," he wrote, "save on the authority of Holy Scripture, since greater is that authority than all the powers of human understanding."

That dictum is the charter of priestly usurpation. It made the centuries in which the Christian Church controlled the civilized world the "dark ages." It burned Bruno at the stake; it put the church in the mortifying position of being compelled to accept, in each new generation, the truths for which it had persecuted devoted men in the preceding generation. It still is dominant in the minds of large numbers and, only a few months ago in Dayton, Tennessee, it produced the trial of a young teacher named Scopes.

Without burdening our rapid survey by too much detail, let us glance for a moment at the unhappy consequences of the idea that God had revealed Himself only in times past, as against the much more inspiring faith that His revelation is continuous.

The Bible is authority for the scientific information that four angels will descend from Heaven and stand upon the four corners of the earth; that Joshua made the sun to stand still; that the waters are let down upon the earth by God and His angels through the "windows of Heaven," and that "It is He that sitteth upon the circle of the earth . . . that stretcheth out the heavens like a curtain, and spreadeth them out like a tent to dwell in."

Proceeding upon this information, the Egyptian monk, Cosmas Indicopleustes, in the sixth century worked out a definite plan of the universe, describing it as a vast box divided into two compartments, the one above the other. In the lower compartment were men; above were God and His angels whose business it was to arrange the stars, and push the sun and moon back and forth across the heavens. A huge mountain at one end concealed the sun during the night.

"We say therefore with Isaiah that the heaven embracing the universe is a vault," Cosmas concluded, "with Job, that it is joined to the earth, and with Moses that the length of the earth is greater than its breadth." He adds that angels and prophets agreed in this definition, and that God, at the last judgment, would send to hell all who questioned it.

This plain and simple system of astronomy was elaborated upon by the devout of succeeding centuries, but not changed in any important detail. All attacks upon it were denounced as atheistic. The constantly recurring suggestion that the earth might be round instead of flat was determinedly resented. St. Gregory Nazianzen showed conclusively that men could never sail beyond Gibraltar, and the pious Lactantius demanded: "Is there any one so senseless as to believe that there are men whose

footsteps are higher than their heads? . . . that
the crops and trees grow downward . . . that
the rains and snow and hail fall upward toward
the earth? . . . I am at a loss what to say of
those who, when they have once erred, steadily
persevere in their folly and defend one vain thing
by another."

To which the great Augustine added his
powerful authority, pointing out that there can
not be men on the other side of the globe, since
"Scripture speaks of no such descendants of
Adam"; since the Psalms, echoed by St. Paul,
say of the preachers of the Gospel that "their
line is gone out through all the earth, and their
words to the end of the world," and since we
know that these preachers did not go to the other
antipodes it is certain, said the Saint, that there
can be no antipodes. They who question this
statement of geographical fact "give the lie
direct to King David and to St. Paul and therefore to the Holy Ghost."

Even in spite of such awful warnings the in-
quiring spirit of humanity would not be
downed. In the early sixteenth century a
simple, plain-speaking professor on the borders
of Poland conceived and announced that the
sun and planets did not revolve about the earth
but that the earth revolved about the sun. His

name was Nicholas Copernicus. He did not make the announcement very loudly. Indeed, so sure was he of the wrath and persecution of the church that he withdrew from his professorship in Rome and kept his great thought to himself and a few trusted associates for thirty years. Finally, knowing that he was close to the end of his days, he dedicated his great work, *Revolutions of the Heavenly Bodies,* to the Pope and entrusted it to a printer. The printer, terror-stricken, brought it out with an apologetic and groveling preface. A copy was carried to the home of Copernicus on May 24, 1543, but the scholar was on his death bed. A few hours later he had passed beyond the reach of those who would have persecuted him and perhaps have taken his life. He had feared that even the grave might not be strong enough to shield his body and so he directed that his tombstone should make no mention of his scientific achievements, but have graven on it merely this pitiful prayer:

"I ask not the grace accorded to Paul; not that given to Peter; give me only the favour which Thou didst show to the thief on the cross."

For years the truth lay buried in the minds of

men too timid to utter it, but finally there arose
one brave enough to speak even within the hearing of the Pope. Giordano Bruno is one of the
strange and fascinating characters of history.
He was hunted from land to land, trapped in
Venice, imprisoned for six years in the dungeons
of the Inquisition at Rome, then burned alive
and his ashes scattered to the winds. Surely
this would be the end of heresy. No man would
any more dare to suggest that the world was
round and moved about the sun.

Yet ten years later Galileo spoke. His announcement was a dramatic fulfilment of
prophecy. Years before, Copernicus had been
confronted with the objection: "If your doctrines were true, Venus would show phases like
the moon." To which the devout old hero had
replied: "You are right; I know not what to
say; but God is good and will in time find an
answer to this objection." Galileo's discovery
was God's answer. His rude little telescope had
revealed the phases of Venus.

The roar of abuse which this discovery pro-
voked was made more bitter by Galileo's subsequent discovery of the mountains and valleys of
the moon, and his deduction that the moon
shines by the reflected light of the sun. The
impiety of this statement is easily proved by the

verse in Genesis which describes the moon as "a great light."

As the implications of Galileo's findings became more clearly understood, the whole theological world rocked with vituperation and abuse. If the earth were not the center of the universe, as theology claimed, but only one of many planets, then these others must be inhabited, since God makes nothing in vain. "Such a thought," said one of the faithful, "would upset the whole basis of theology. If the earth is a planet, and only one among several planets, it can not be that any such great things have been done specially for it, as the Christian doctrine teaches. . . . If there be other planets . . . how can their inhabitants be descended from Adam? How can they trace their origin to Noah's ark? How can they have been redeemed by the Saviour?"

Hot and bitter was the warfare: Galileo on one side, alone, and against him all the organized power of the church. In 1616 he was summoned before the Inquisition at Rome, where the theologians examined him, pondered his doctrines for a month, and then gave forth their verdict.

"The first proposition, that the sun is the center and does not revolve about the earth, is foolish, absurd, false in theology, and heretical, because expressly contrary to Holy Scripture," and "the second proposition, that the earth is not the center, but revolves about the sun, is absurd, false in philosophy, and from a theological point of view at least, opposed to the true faith."

Threatened with the dungeons of the Inquisition, Galileo agreed to conform, and for years neither published nor taught. But when a new Pope came to the throne, Urban VIII, a cultured man with greater promise of intelligence, he took courage and began to profess his faith again. Alas, Urban was no more openminded than his predecessor. Haled again before the Inquisition and threatened with torture, Galileo was compelled to sign that bitter recantation which has come down through the ages.

"I, Galileo, being in my seventieth year, being a prisoner and on my knees, and before your Eminences, having before my eyes the Holy Gospel, which I touch with my hands, abjure, curse and detest the error and the heresy of the movement of the earth."

Seventy years old he was, and his recantation spared his life. But it did not gain his freedom nor liberate him from abuse. To the end of his days he was confined and annoyed until, blind, wasted and pitiful, he passed away. Even then the persecution did not cease. His petition that he be buried in his family tomb, was denied. His friends wished to erect a monument over him, but their desire was thwarted by the Pope.

"It would be an evil example for the world," said the Holy Father, "if such honors were rendered to a man who had been brought before the Roman Inquisition for an opinion so false and erroneous; who had communicated it to so many others and who had given so great a scandal to Christendom."

Alone, apart from his family, he was cast into an ignoble grave, and not for a hundred years did the hostility of the theologians relent sufficiently to allow his remains to be removed to a worthy tomb and a monument erected over them.

The persecutors of Copernicus and Galileo, the burners of Bruno, were Catholics, for the Catholic Church was in power. But let no one assume that Protestants were more tolerant or that, given the authority, they would have acted otherwise.

Said Luther: "People gave ear to an upstart astrologer (Copernicus) who strove to show that the earth revolves, not the heavens or the firmament, the sun and the moon. . . . This fool wishes to reverse the entire science of astronomy; but sacred Scripture tells us that Joshua commanded the sun to stand still, and not the earth."

To which Melancthon, the mildest of the reformers, added eight proofs that "the earth can be nowhere if not in the center of the universe," and suggested that such teachings as those of Copernicus merited the severest penalties.

For hundred of years the world was held back because theologians contended that God had put all He knew into one single old book and would never send fresh revelations to men. Even the purest Christian characters, Isaac Newton, Pascal, Locke, Milton, were denounced as "atheists" and "infidels." And Descartes, whose proofs of the existence of God have been a powerful influence on millions of modern minds, would have been tortured to death by the Protestants of Holland if they could have laid their hands on him, and was thwarted throughout his life by the Catholics of France and denied decent honors after his death.

The story of the struggle would be humorous if it were not so tragic. Always science was just a step ahead. Always the church was in the sad necessity of having to admit what it had just denounced, with its infallible authority, as untrue. Carefully worked out theological proofs were hardly arrived at before something happened to unsettle them.

Thus Dr. John Lightfoot, Vice Chancellor of the University of Cambridge and one of the most learned Hebrew scholars of his time, after a painful searching of the Scriptures announced that "heaven and earth, center and circumference, were created all together, in the same instant, and clouds full of water," and that "this work took place and man was created by the Trinity on October 23, 4004 B. C., at nine o'clock in the morning."

A great discovery indeed. Yet less than two centuries later the spades of explorers in Egypt revealed the fact that a very cultivated people, enjoying most of the comforts of modern civilization, were dwelling peacefully upon the shores of the Nile many decades before Doctor Lightfoot's date of creation.

In so brief a survey as this we can not go further with the age-long controversy. Those who would follow it in detail will enjoy the *History of the Warfare of Science with Theology* by Dr. Andrew D. White, a great treatise from which we, like other subsequent writers on the subject, have made liberal borrowings. Enough has been written here to show the broad outlines of the long and losing battle. Fearing change, terror-stricken lest some new discovery might rock the ancient structures, organized religion in all countries has denied and threatened, and tortured and slain. With so bad a record, is it entitled to survive? Are the services rendered great enough to overbalance this awful debit? Is any institution which has shown itself so unadaptable, so lacking in appreciation of the expanding life of the intellect, fitted to be useful in this modern, pulsing world?

To these questions five honest answers can be made.

First of all, when the Roman government went down before the Goths and Vandals there was one agency of civilization, and only one, which was strong enough to survive. That one was the Christian Church. Whatever of art and scholarship, whatever of idealism and faith, lived through those recurring catastrophes was saved by the care and sacrifice of priests and monks and nuns. If the church was responsible for darkening the Middle Ages by suppressing the full glow of scientific progress, it is equally true that the little spark of learning from which scientists were later to relight their larger torches was preserved not in laboratories or libraries, for there were none, but in the cells of monasteries.

71

The church did more than merely survive. It laid its restraining hand on the savage victors and rescued some salvage for the future. Yes, and even more. It conquered the conquerors; it taught them to worship. Was the work of regeneration superficial? Were the converts still pagan under the skin? Do we even now preserve in Christian ceremonial some things of heathen origin? Unquestionably.

The church suffered as well as gained by its victory. *But it did conquer.* It did turn the tide. The sweeping floods of barbarism that threatened to wipe out all the progress won by centuries of civilized effort were brought under control. Destructive energy was directed into constructive channels. The church alone stood firm when all else tottered. It saved enough of civilization so that the structure could be rebuilt.

We need to remember, in the second place, that history touches only the high spots. It shows us kings and princes, popes and cardinals, ambassadors and generals: their ambitions, intrigues, selfishness and cruelties, and from these allows us to deduce the rest. It does not show us what went on beneath the surface. Far down below these troubled heights there were peaceful valleys of common life. Here, and not upon the unlovely peaks, was the real life of the age. If religion meant only intolerance and bigotry above, it had a different significance below. To the masses it was faith, and encouragement, and comfort, and hope for eternal life.

The Book of Judges in the Old Testament corresponds, in a sense, to the chapters of history which deal with the "dark ages." It is an "in-between" book, bridging the gap from civilized Egypt to the later period of renaissance under David and Solomon. It is filled with ignorance and cruelty. Again and again it apologizes for the horrible deeds recorded, reminding the reader that "there was no king in Israel, and every man did that which was right in his own eyes." You think as you read that it must have been an altogether depraved and hopeless era, as if life could not possibly have been worth the struggle and terror which it cost. But again only the peaks are revealed. Following the Book of Judges comes the Book of Ruth, which begins with this significant sentence: "Now it came to pass in the days when the Judges ruled."

What came to pass? What good things could possibly come to pass in such evil days? Read the answer in the four short chapters that follow. They make one of the sweetest stories in the world.

For "it came to pass in the days when the

judges ruled" that Elimelech was taking good care of his wife and two boys. It came to pass in the terrible days when the judges ruled that those two boys were growing up and marrying good girls and establishing happy homes. It came to pass in the bloody days when the judges ruled that Ruth was standing loyally by her mother-in-law, saying: "Intreat me not to leave thee, . . . for whither thou goest, I will go; and where thou lodgest, I will lodge: thy people shall be my people, and thy God my God."

It came to pass in those awful days that a prosperous man, Boaz, was watching the women who gleaned in his fields, not to betray but to protect them, and he saw Ruth and admired her and married her, and she became the mother of a fine household, and an ancestress of Jesus of Nazareth.

A rather nice set of circumstances to have taken place in those fearful days when the judges ruled.

So in the ages which priesthood helped to make dark there was loyalty and kindliness and simple faith in the humbler ranks of life. And there was genius higher up also, which had its inspiration in the church. There was Fra Angelico, who prayed always before he began a

74

picture. To be sure, his angels were flat-chested and emaciated, but he broke away resolutely from the unearthly ugliness of Byzantine tradition, and the faces of his angels were the faces of pretty women, and their clothes were the best that could be bought in the shops of Florence.

There was Fra Lippo Lippi, who brought art back to nature, still keeping it religious. And there was, most splendid of the characters of the Middle Ages, perhaps the finest spirit that has lived since the days in Palestine—Francis, the Saint of Assisi.

The world can afford to be very forgiving toward a faith, and an institution, that can produce a Francis. Born to wealth, the son of a prosperous merchant and a noble lady, he passed his youth as was expected of a high-bred youngster. He tasted all the pleasures, sinned all the sins, and was a ringleader in revelry. At twenty he was taken prisoner of war and languished for a year behind the bars. The experience left its mark upon a constitution which, never strong, was continually neglected and wore out at the too early age of forty-four. But it left an imprint on his spirit also. He came back into the world with a new idea. Pleasure for itself was a fraud; man was made for something higher than deviltry. The years were meant to be put to noble purposes. One alone had shown how they might be invested best. Francis determined to reproduce in his own life, so far as possible, the life of Jesus.

He turned his back on luxury and "married his Lady Poverty." He set up a rigid discipline over his body. If there was any task which he hated to do, it was his rule to do that thing at once. Lover of comfort and beauty though he was, he made himself the friend of lepers and the outcast. His clothes were the simplest; his food was crusts begged from door to door.

All this was splendid, and men and women rallied to his standard, finding to their surprise that in forgetting themselves they were genuinely more happy than when their days had been entirely selfish. But the most splendid part of it all was that Francis caught the spirit of Jesus in its entirety. Too many of the pious of all ages have been gloomy folk. Jesus was above all a happy man. He loved the crowd. He enjoyed weddings and frequented feasts. Little children flocked to Him, and sick people immediately felt better when He entered the room. Francis shared this joy to the full. He "loved everybody and everything—men in the fields, women in their homes, the little children who flocked to him, the animals who ran to him, the birds to whom he preached, the very worms which he picked up from the dust that they might not be crushed." Men called him "the troubadour of God," and it was easy to know his followers, for they sang as they walked and danced with joy.

I read recently the letter of a former missionary to China who related his debate with a cultured Chinese official. He presented as ably as he could the superior claims of Christianity, and the Chinaman listened with polite attention. When the missionary had finished, the Chinaman arose and took down a book from the shelves and handed it to the missionary.

"How strange it is," he said, "that your great prophet Jesus should, in all the centuries, have made but one convert." He pointed to the book, and the missionary, looking down at it, saw that it was a biography of St. Francis.

Every age has had its quota of St. Francises. I saw one once, a benign, kindly old gentleman named John G. Paton. He spoke to a church full of people, and his talk was much more modest, more self-effacing than his hearers could have wished. They plied him with questions afterward, trying to induce him to give more details of his extraordinary experience, for they knew the larger outlines of the story.

WHAT CAN A MAN BELIEVE?

Alone, without support or influence, but moved by a youthful enthusiasm, he had stepped out of a boat and walked up the sandy shore of an island in the New Hebrides. No other white men had visited that shore, unless in armed bands, or, occasionally, a sailor from a shipwrecked vessel. Luckless sailor! The inhabitants were cannibals of the most savage type. Every castaway had been cooked and eaten. The islands were certain death to white men. Paton had been fully warned; his end was absolutely sure. Yet, without a weapon, with nothing but a Bible in his hand, he walked in among the savages. And so began the civilization of the New Hebrides.

I saw another St. Francis in Boston, a white whiskered old man with one of the kindest faces in the world. All his life he had lived and worked among the poorest of that city. In all the years his mind had known hardly a single thought about himself. And his eyes showed it.

I asked him: "How do you live? Who provides for your food and clothes, since you give all your little income away? Aren't you worried about what will happen when you are too feeble to work?"

For answer he pulled out a little slip of paper and passed it over to me.

"There is my assurance of income," he said. "That's a promissory note signed by the Owner of the universe. Who can be afraid with a promise like that?"

This was the note:

"Trust in the Lord and do good. So shalt thou dwell in the land, and *verily thou shalt be fed.*"

There has not been one St. Francis. There have been thousands of them. Some have turned their backs on the entanglements and problems of ordinary life and devoted their whole energy to religious service. The larger number have attained their sublime characters through the duties and sacrifices of the common lot. These latter have left no record on the pages of history, but they have passed faith down through the ages. Because of them we can forgive the cruelties of popes, the excesses of Luther, the burning of Servetus by Calvin, the bloody trail of inquisitions and "holy" wars. Despite the terrible shortcomings of the church, the noblest spirits of all ages have somehow found their inspiration in it. Their lives are its atonement.

Those institutions in our modern life which we look on as the best fruits of civilization had their roots—almost all of them—in the church. This is the fourth thing which must be set down to its credit.

At the very tip of Cape Cod rises a conspicuous monument erected both to commemorate a notable event and to serve as a guide for vessels bound for the ports of Boston or New York. The event was the signing of the Mayflower Compact. The Pilgrims had not expected to need any such compact. They carried to this new continent a charter from the Crown authorizing them to found a colony in "the northern parts of Virginia," which meant New Jersey. But the *Mayflower* had been driven from her course by winter gales and was too much weakened to undertake the further voyage. They must land near where they were, as they did a few days later at Plymouth; and, since they believed that their charter was valueless in this part of the country, something had to be provided in its place. Already discontent had shown itself on the little boat. Some of the passengers were hired servants who began to say that, since the charter was void, they were no longer compelled to work their passage or be obedient to orders. Some sort of government must be established, and at once.

The Pilgrims learned all this on Friday

night, November 10, 1620, Old Style, or November 20, New Style. On Saturday morning they assembled every man on the *Mayflower,* except two or three who died a few days later and may be presumed to have been too sick to attend. Forty-one men, the minister and the magistrate, the freeman and the indentured servant, and every one signed the Compact. Their authority was stated to be "by these presents," which means by their free voice and equal vote.

Under that simple Compact they organized their little army, legislated as to the ownership of shares in the red cow when she arrived, established limits within which roofs should not be made of thatch and thus imperil other buildings, settled small disagreements, and, when a murder was committed by one of their own number, summoned a jury, gave the culprit a fair trial, and sentenced him to be hanged by the neck until dead. Thus seriously did they later regard their act in creating a government. And the whole thing was done in a few hours. Between Friday night and Saturday noon, there in the cabin of the *Mayflower,* the machinery was set up and put in operation.

Where had they learned the science of statecraft? Who had taught them to carry an empire in their brains and bring it forth full-fledged at a moment's notice?

Theodore Roosevelt, in laying the corner-stone of the Pilgrim Monument, expressed amazement at the feat and asked the questions without being able to answer them. William Howard Taft, in dedicating the monument three years later, showed in his speech that he had given the Compact much more careful study than his predecessor, but he also expressed the same amazement. But on each occasion there was a second speaker: Senator Henry Cabot Lodge at the corner-stone laying, and President Charles W. Eliot of Harvard at the dedication. These two men gently corrected the failure of the two Presidents to understand. They answered the question: "Where and how did the Pilgrims learn to create a ready-made democracy?"

Said Doctor Eliot: "Although the signing of the Compact was a sudden act, caused by the refusal of the captain of the *Mayflower* on the day before to take his vessel through the danger-ous shoals which lie off the southeastern coast of Massachusetts, and so to bring it to the Hud-son River, where the English charter obtained by the Pilgrims before leaving Leyden authorized them to establish their colony, *it was an act which their whole experience of their church in England and in Holland, and the essence of the doctrines taught by their pastor and elders, naturally led up to.*"

He went on to quote a paragraph from the teaching of the Pilgrim minister, Reverend John Robinson, and said:

"The whole doctrine and method of cooperative good will can not be better stated to-day. . . . Everything that is good in modern socialism is contained in that single sentence, and nothing of the bad or foolish."

In other words, our American democratic institutions which we cherish with so much pride came not from statesmen or business executives but from church conferences and prayer meetings, from the long continued practise of the Pilgrims in choosing their own pastors, fixing their own conditions of membership, and managing generally their own church affairs.

Our higher education came to us from the same source. Stop for a moment before the gates of Harvard and read the inscription copied from a quaint old document called "New England's First Fruits":

"After God had carried us safe to New England, and wee had bilded our houses, provided necessaries for our livli-hood, rear'd convenient places for Gods worship, and settled the civill government; one of the next things we longed for, and looked after was to advance *learning* and perpetuate it to posterity; dreading to leave an illiterate ministry to the churches, when our present ministers shall lie in the dust."

A few ministers coming together, and each of them giving a few books—this was how Harvard College began. Education in America did not start with some millionaire donating a stadium; it started with a sincere hope that learning and religious leadership might be preserved. The charter said that Harvard was founded to promote "the advancement of all good literature, arts and sciences," and the "education of English and Indian youth in knowledge and godliness."

The five great historic New England colleges for men—Harvard, Yale, Amherst, Williams, Dartmouth; the three historic schools for women—Mount Holyoke, Wellesley and Smith—all grew out of the same impulse. And so did the colleges that went with the westward march of civilization toward the Pacific Coast.

If democracy and modern education are the gifts of the church, so also are hospitals for the sick and insane, and all the multitude of agencies for social service in which our civilization has so much pride. "And, as ye go," said Jesus of Nazareth, "preach, saying, The kingdom of Heaven is at hand. Heal the sick, cleanse the lepers, raise the dead, cast out devils; freely ye have received; freely give." His message was a twofold gospel—good news for the body as well as the soul. For a long time the healing portion of the command was considerably neglected. But some centuries before the crusades certain rich and pious merchants of Amalfi were distressed because many people who made pilgrimages to the Holy Land trusted the Lord for everything, including even the common-sense necessities which they ought to have provided for themselves, and so suffered from poverty and sickness. These Christian merchants determined to establish a hospital and hotel at Jerusalem for poor sick pilgrims. The twin institutions were dedicated to St. John the Almoner, and later to St. John the Baptist, patron saint of the Knights of St. John.

With the coming of the crusades these institutions, and the Order which supported them, became one of the most famous of Christian institutions. The Knights were not content to heal wounds, to be sure; they sallied forth to inflict a few on the Saracens—but this is no part of our present story. The point is that the first people in all the world who ever took it into their heads to establish special care for the sick and unfortunate were Christian men, inspired by the teaching of Him who said: "Inasmuch as ye have done it unto one of the least of these my brethren, ye have done it unto me."

Later on in this little book we shall have something to say of the other great religions and how each of them has discovered a magnificent part of the same big truth. We shall ask the question: Which, of all these various faiths, is the best? And we shall find much to be said in favor of the teachings of the gentle Buddha, of the serene Confucius, and even of the vigorous Mohammed. But we shall not find a record of the followers of any of these religions going forth on to battle-fields at the risk of their lives to ease the pain of friends and foes alike. Only Christianity rises to that height. The American Red Cross is not ostensibly a religious organization. But who was Clara Barton, its founder? I saw her in our home when I was a lad, a quiet and forceful little woman, a distant relative of mine. She made no parade of her religion and hardly admitted that she had a creed. But she had one. And the symbol of the organization which she founded was and is the Cross.

So there are these four honest things to be

said on the side of the church, as against the
record of bigotry and selfishness with which too
many of its official pages are indelibly stained:
(1) It alone stood firm through vandal in-
vasions and salvaged enough to provide
foundations for a new civilization; (2) through
all the ages it has been faith and kindliness and
the hope of immortality to the submerged
millions; (3) through all the ages it has inspired
the finest characters, the sweetest spirits; (4) it
gave us our democracy, our higher education,
and the tender impulses on which physicians and
legislators and social workers have erected their
works for the suffering and the poor.

To these four counts we add a final fifth.
The church is the one institution in the modern
world whose sole business is to create in men
dissatisfaction with their own characters, their
achievements and ideals.

It is not strange, when you think of it, that
more people do not go to church. The amazing
thing is that anybody goes. What is it that they
go for? To be told that they are sinful. To be
asked to give money for poor and sick and unfortunate people whom they have never seen,
and who have no claim of blood relationship
upon them. To be sent away dissatisfied with
all that they are or have done in comparison

with what Jesus was and did. The wonder, I say, is not that more do not attend but that any human beings at all should voluntarily submit themselves, Sunday after Sunday, to the reminder that they can and should do better than they have done.

This ceaseless insistence that humanity is capable of better things; this unrelenting challenge to higher thinking, nobler action, more unselfish living—this makes the church a great constructive power, whatever its follies of over-organization, its pettiness of creed. It lives in one sense from hand to mouth. It prays day by day for its daily bread, and feeds every Sunday out of the contribution box. It has only so much as is cheerfully given to it. Yet it has assets, even financial ones, greater than Standard Oil or United States Steel or any other commercial enterprise. Its missions, its hospitals, its colleges bring no revenue, but are, on the contrary, a daily source of huge expense. Yet they live by faith and grow as the church discovers in each new generation a certain company of unselfish folks who respond to its call to sacrifice.

Such an institution, in spite of mistakes and shortcomings, will not die; and could not, at any cost, be spared. It may change, I believe, very

radically from its present type and characteristics. In a later chapter we shall have something to say about the possible forms which those
changes may take. But it will be much easier for
liberal-minded men to graft new life on to the old
institution than to discard it. Indeed, it can not
be discarded. Those who believe it can be speak
with singularly little knowledge of history or
of the deep cravings of the human heart. The
hymn writer was a better historian and a sounder
psychologist :

> "Oh, where are kings and empires now
>   Of old that went and came?
> But Lord, thy church is praying yet,
>   A thousand years the same."

CHAPTER III

THE twelve hundred years between 600 B. C. and 600 A. D. seem to have been the most propitious for starting religions. In that comparatively brief period four faiths were founded—Buddhism, Confucianism, Christianity and Mohammedanism—which enroll several hundred million members of the human race. They were launched into the world by four great personalities. What was the life of each of these leaders? What did he teach? Wherein did his teaching differ from that of the others? And which of the four taught best?

BUDDHA

There was uncertainty as to the date and place of Buddha's birth until 1895, when an English archeologist discovered a pillar erected by the Emperor Asoka, that splendid prince whom H. G. Wells regards as one of the six greatest men who ever lived. This discovery fixed the date at about 560 B. C., and the place as near Kapilavastu, whose ruins lie in the wilderness beyond the British borders of North India. The little brown boy, whose coming brought so much happiness to a very wealthy father and mother, was named Siddhartha Gautama, but his subsequent title of Buddha, "the enlightened," has displaced his own name in much the same way that the title Christ has displaced the name of Jesus.

Many years later a vast body of tradition gathered around Gautama, and this has been added to through the centuries until it is difficult to find the truth. It was said that his mother had been impregnated by the light of a star, and that earthquakes marked his entry into the world, and miracles of healing. Gentle rains fell in seasons that according to the calendar should have been dry; flowers bloomed in abundance where summer heat should have withered all plant life, and the normal course of events was generally upset.

His rajah father, ambitious to have his son succeed to the family estates, was disturbed by the thirty-two portents that accompanied the birth and, fearing that the lad would be a monk, sought by every inducement to make him a permanent part of the life to which he had been born. The boy grew strong; he was preeminent in athletic contests, as well as in his studies. One of the stories of his youth may be legendary but it is so much in harmony with his later character that it deserves preservation.

His cousin shot a swan, which fell among the roses in the garden. Gautama rescued the bird and pulled the arrow from the wound. He had never known pain; to learn its nature he pricked his own wrist with the arrow and felt the sting and saw the flowing blood, and his heart went out toward all suffering of man and beast. Then and there he dedicated himself, in an early and pre-enlightened fashion, to the relief of pain.

The story says that his cousin demanded the bird, but Gautama refused to give it up. Whereupon they submitted the question to the wise men of the district, and one aged man, who had never been seen among them before, announced that if the power to destroy life might be assumed to give the cousin a right to the swan, much more did the power and will to save life confer the ownership on him who had preserved it. When the other wise men looked around to see who it was that had spoken they could not discover the prophet, but a snake glided away. Thus the gods sometimes disappeared when they had performed their mission.

WHICH IS THE BEST RELIGION?

It was Gautama's skill in archery that won the willing heart of the Princess Yasôdhara, to whom he was married at the age of nineteen. The father provided three luxurious palaces, one for each of the three Indian seasons, and there would seem to have been nothing for the young people to desire. Yet Gautama was not happy. Passing along the road one day, he saw four appalling sights—a decrepit old man, a man loathsomely sick, a corpse and a monk. The last was in some respects the most terrible of all, a religious ascetic intent only on achieving his own salvation through self-discipline and utterly undisturbed by the sorrows of the world. Gautama became distressed at the thought that he, and all mankind, were destined to the miseries of sickness, old age and death, and that the current philosophies were powerless to give peace.

He made his decision. Slipping away at night from his beautiful wife and his new-born child, he renounced his throne and fortune, and fled on his white horse Kantaka, accompanied by a single servant. The prince of evil, Mara, sought to restrain him, but he was proof against temptation. On the farther side of a stream he dismissed his servant, sent back his horse, and went forth in beggar's clothes to find a solution of life's enigma.

WHAT CAN A MAN BELIEVE?

It is said there were sixty-two schools in India at that time, most of them teaching the attainment of holiness by asceticism. Gautama went to Alara Kalama, whose fame was wide.

"Thus vowed to homelessness and seeking the highest, even the way of peace, I went where the ascetic Alara Kalama dwelt and thus addressed him, 'Friend Kalama, I would lead the life of a recluse as your pupil and follower.' And very swiftly I learned, O disciples, what he had to teach."

What he learned was the "eight stages of meditation"—self-mortification raised to the n-th degree. He gave it a thorough trial.

"Like wasted withered reeds became all my limbs, like a camel's hoof my hip, like a wavy rope my backbone, and as in a ruined house the roof-tree rafters show all aslope, so sloping showed my ribs because of the extremity of fasting. As in a deep well the watery gleam far below is scarcely to be seen, so in my eye-sockets the gleam of my eye-balls far sunken well nigh disappeared, and as a severed gourd becomes rotten and shrunken when left out in the sun and uncooked, so hollow and shrunken became the skin of my head. When I touched the surface of my belly my hand touched the backbone, and as I stroked my flesh, the hair, rotten at the roots, came away in my hands."

Hundreds of others who were seeking the pure life could have duplicated all these particulars, and some of them professed to find peace, but not Gautama. He later characterized asceticism as "the realm of nothingness." Self-denial he still believed to be the way of enlightenment but not self-torture. This was his famous "middle way" between self-indulgence and self-immolation. It was what many counted a heresy, but it insured his success.

At the end of the sixth year of searching he sat for six days under the Bo tree, and in that week there came to him the bliss of emancipation.

Another week he spent under a goatherd's banyan tree. There he was asked to define the true characteristics of a Brahman, which reminds us that Buddhism did not begin as an independent religion, but was a sect of Brahmanism as Christianity in the beginning was a sect of Judaism. The now enlightened Gautama replied that the Brahman should be free from pride, free from impurity, should be self-reliant and wise, having fulfilled the requirements of holiness.

A third week was passed under the Muchalinda tree, where Muchalinda, the serpent king, came forth and spread his hood as a canopy to protect Gautama from the sun and rain.

WHAT CAN A MAN BELIEVE?

The final week was under the Rajayatana tree, and here two merchants came bringing honey and rice cakes. The food was presented in four bowls of stone by the four divinities that guard the four quarters of the earth. Gautama ate gladly. His long struggle was at an end. He was enlightened.

The title Buddha had belonged to many men before his time, as the title Messiah or Christ had belonged to all the Davidic kings and others, including Saul. With his "enlightenment," Gautama became a Buddha. While other Buddhas are expected, and the greatest of all is yet to come, he stood and yet stands so far above all others as almost to monopolize the title.

Like Christianity, Buddhism has its sacred books; its gospel is based on the Four Noble Truths which came while he sat cross-legged under the Bo tree:

All existence involves suffering. Suffering is caused by desire. The path to a cessation of suffering is the eightfold path of right living. Suffering will cease when desire ceases.

These Four Noble Truths were elaborated in this fashion:

The suffering to which all existence is subject is fourfold. Suffering attends birth, decay, disease, death.

Suffering may be defined in four ways:

The presence of objects we hate is suffering.
The absence of things we love is suffering.
Not to obtain what we desire is suffering.
The clinging to existence is suffering.

The eightfold path to cessation of suffering is by right belief, right aspiration, right speech, right conduct, right occupation, right endeavor, right memory, right meditation. The perfect condition is Nirvana, in which desire is totally extinct. While one lives the goal is to approach as nearly as possible to a condition free from desire.

All this is a far cry from the doctrine of self-mortification. Buddha did not teach self-torture as the means to a holy life, but distinctly revolted from it. He had tried that in his six years of struggle, and his success was like the effort to tie knots in the air.

For a time he considered whether it was worth while to waste these truths on an unappreciative world. There was little in them to attract the heedless. Even self-torture has an element of delight in the degree to which one may comfort his soul at the expense of the suffering of his body, and perhaps the added joy of being admired as a holy man; but the quiet life of subdued desire has little appeal to any sense of the heroic. So Buddha did not rush out to spread his doctrine. But the two merchants who brought him food after his four weeks under the trees became his first lay converts, and others followed. Gradually he moved farther out into the suffering world, carrying his message of the elimination of pain by the elimination of desire, a doctrine which necessarily forbids the infliction of pain on others.

New disciples came until there were hundreds who wore the yellow robe and followed him in a fellowship of free democracy. He even permitted, after a threefold refusal, an order of women disciples.

"Their admission means that the Good Law shall not endure for a thousand years but only for five hundred," he said. "For as when the mildew falls on a field the rice is doomed, so when women leave the household life and join an Order, that Order will not long endure. Yet as water is held by a strong dyke, so I have established a barrier of regulations which are not to be transgressed."

He held out no promise of ease or comfort. The disciples slept on the ground with no cover but the yellow robe. He could have said, and did say in effect: "If any man will come after me, let him take up the cross."

Lepers and maimed men were not admitted to his fellowship, nor yet slaves or confirmed criminals, but every other class came, from nobles to mendicants. Often they quarreled and made trouble, but however much they disagreed among themselves their loyalty to him never wavered. In time rich estates were given, and he and his followers walked in cool groves, which he dearly loved, but they maintained their simple living. He himself went forth at every dawn to beg his food for the day, and more and more the common people, to say nothing of kings and courtesans, counted it an honor to bestow bread upon him.

What he gave his followers was hardly a religion. He taught them almost nothing about God, prayer, forgiveness, or a future life. His was a way of holiness through self-denial, as opposed to self-torture on the one hand and self-indulgence on the other. Later, his disciples wrought this simple teaching into an intricate system of metaphysics and dogma which took on new forms as the religion spread.

China was the first mission field. About 61 A. D., while the books of the New Testament were being written and nine years before Jerusalem was destroyed by Titus, the Chinese

WHAT CAN A MAN BELIEVE?

Emperor Ming-ti had a dream in consequence of which he sent to India and imported Buddhist priests. Six years were spent in the translation of Buddhist books into Chinese, and the new religion was taking root in China just about the time the siege of Jerusalem was scattering Christians as missionaries all over Asia Minor, Greece and Egypt. In this new environment a religion without gods or worship could not satisfy, so the worship of Buddha himself, already begun in India, was transported and made rapid headway.

Six hundred years later Japan imported Buddhism. Colossal statues of Buddha were erected, and two of them still stand. The goddess of mercy, Kwannon, is often in the same temple, and there is a collection of minor gods sufficient for all the real or imaginary needs of the Japanese mind. There is prayer also, and provision for its mechanical continuity through prayer-wheels run by air or water power. And the doctrine and ritual are bewilderingly involved.

This intricacy of idol worship would scandalize Buddha, who never proclaimed himself an object of adoration and indeed taught very little about worship in any form. The earlier and simpler narratives show him very clearly for just what he was—a friendly, compassionate, but very human man.

"The Blessed One was troubled with wind on his stomach.

"Now when the Blessed One had eaten food prepared by Kunda, the worker in metal, there fell upon him a dire sickness, the disease of dysentery; and a sharp pain came upon him, even unto death."

He made no pretense. He never claimed to have attained perfection, and freely acknowledged four weaknesses, one of which was too much love of wine. He asked nothing of life except peace through self-forgetfulness and kindliness to others. He might have been a king. He might have molded his followers into an army and conquered vast territories. All this power and wealth and luxury he renounced to set an example of unselfish goodness. Said he to his first sixty disciples:

"Go ye now out of compassion for the world, for the welfare of gods and men. Let not two of you go the same way. Preach the doctrine which is glorious. Proclaim a consummate, perfect and pure life of holiness."

They were obedient to his command. But their successors carried a very different message.

101

They proclaimed Buddha a god, and erected an institution which, with its wealth and ritual and forms, is as far from his character and ideals as darkness is from light. But it lives and grows and serves, after its fashion, to represent religion to some hundreds of millions of human souls.

CONFUCIUS

The real name of Confucius was his family name, Kung. He was called Kung the Master, Kung Fu Tze. That combination of syllables was too difficult for European tongues, and so it was Latinized into the form with which we are familiar. The great teacher was born in Shantung in 551 B. C., and died there in 478, and his grave is one of the sacred shrines of China.

What we know about him is contained in twenty small books called the *Analects,* recording conversations with his disciples, and certain other descriptive and biographical matter. There is some material also in another book, *Doctrine of the Mean.*

His father, Shuh-liang Heih, a military officer, was seventy years old at the time of his birth and had ten children, but Confucius, the youngest, was the only able-bodied son. His birth, as embellished by later admirers, was accompanied by divine portents. Genii announced to Yen Ching-tsai, his mother, the approaching hour of her deliverance, and fairies attended the cradle.

He appears to have been reared in poverty and to have been self-educated. We are told that he played at the arrangement of vessels and at postures of ceremony, which would seem to show an innate love of ritual. He was an earnest student of history. At the age of fifteen he "bent his mind to learning," and at nineteen he was married. The marriage appears not to have been a happy one. There is a tradition that he divorced his wife; we know for certain that he reproved his son in later years for mourning her death.

The relations between Confucius and this only son were not intimate. When the boy became one of his father's students his fellow disciples were eager to know whether he was learning more than the rest of them.

"Have you heard any lessons from your father in addition to those he has taught us?" one of them asked.

"No," replied the boy. "He was standing alone when I passed with hasty steps through the court below, and he asked me: 'Have you read the Odes?' On my replying, 'Not yet,' he said to me: 'If you do not learn the Odes you will not be fit to converse with.' Another day in the same place and the same way he asked me: 'Have you read the Rules of Propriety?' On my replying, 'Not yet,' he said: 'If you do not read the Rules of Propriety your character can not be established.' "

The enthusiastic fellow pupil exclaimed: "I asked one thing and you have told me three. I now know about the Odes, and I have learned about the Rules of Propriety, and I have learned that the Superior Man maintains a distant reserve towards his son."

We are not informed concerning the reason for this reserve, and it is difficult to reconcile with Confucius' own theory of parental behavior. For he held that if a son did not honor his father the father was probably as much to blame for it as the son. At one time when he was in an official position under Duke Ting of Loo, a father brought a charge of unfilial conduct against his own boy. Confucius caused them both to be imprisoned for three months. He was about to release them when he was asked why he did not put the son to death instead, and he replied: "The father who does not teach his son his duties is equally guilty with the son who neglects them."

He held a similar theory with regard to the

State. Human nature, he said, was inherently good. If the State did not produce good citizens, it reaped the harvest of its own bad sowing. "Let the government be good and the people will be good."

The native state of Confucius, Loo by name, was in North China, on the Yellow River, and is included in the present province of Shantung. There he grew to manhood and mainly spent his life. About the time of his marriage he obtained a small government post, first as keeper of stores of grain and later as guardian of the public fields and lands. But he did not hold these positions long. At the age of twenty-two he was released from official responsibility and became a teacher.

He received all pupils who came to him, no matter how small the tuition price which they were able to bring. He who came with "a bundle of dried fish," the cheapest of all national products, was welcomed as heartily as the student who brought an adequate fee. But he had little patience with those who were not in earnest.

"I do not open the truth to one who is not eager for knowledge. Nor do I help one who is not anxious to explain himself. When I have presented one corner of a subject, and the listener can not from that unfold the other three, I do not repeat my lesson."

He taught a well rounded curriculum, his three principal subjects being history, poetry and literature. After these came four others, proprieties, government, natural science and music. He had pride in those pupils who displayed virtuous, oratorical, administrative or literary abilities, but he avoided feats of strength, prodigies, disorder and the supernatural.

Confucius was devoted to the founders of the Chow dynasty. In a spirit of great reverence he visited the royal capital and returned, not disillusioned by what he saw of political power, but rather strengthened in his veneration for the government. But it was not so with his respect for Lao Tze, the founder of Taoism, whom he visited on this same journey.

Lao Tze was about fifty years older than Confucius, and promulgated a soft, sweet gospel that offered no cure for the problems of the world. He was a pacifist, withdrawing himself from evils which he could not prevent and toward which he could assume only an attitude of imperturbable meekness.

Confucius went to see this venerable man who, according to the Taoist traditions, read to the ardent young teacher a lofty lecture, the burden of which was advice to cease meddling with matters which were beyond his control. It was

106

characteristic of Confucius that he did not reply, but the advice of Lao Tze was lost on him. He was a practical man; Lao Tze was a dealer in sweetness and light. So the two eminent teachers parted and never met again, and the two systems developed side by side and neither gave much aid or comfort to the other.

It was a part of the method of Confucius not to answer back.

"A sage will not enter a tottering state nor dwell in a disorganized one. Where right principles of government prevail, he shows himself, but when they are prostituted he conceals himself.

"The ancients were guarded in their speech. Like them we should avoid loquacity. Many words invite many defeats. Avoid entering many businesses, for many businesses create many difficulties."

These were not original precepts with him, but when he saw them in an inscription on the back of a statue with a triple clasp upon the mouth of the man, he applauded it.

"Observe this, my children. These words are true, and commend themselves to our reason."

WHAT CAN A MAN BELIEVE?

The Duke of Tse had been a patron of the teacher and offered him a pension. Confucius could have used the money to good advantage but he refused the gift.

He said to his disciples: "A superior man will only receive reward for services which he has done. I have given advice to the Duke of Tse, and he has not obeyed it; yet now he would bestow on me this gratuity. He is very far from understanding me."

This incident shows his high superiority to bribes or perquisites. He maintained, even in poverty, a resolute independence. He was determined to be what he talked so much about, a "superior man."

For thirty years, from the time he was twenty-one till he was fifty-one, he was a successful teacher, with a large and reverent band of students. In 500 B. C., he was appointed magistrate and then promoted to be assistant superintendent of public works, and later, a minister of justice. These were high positions and enabled him to test out his theories with success. But jealousy and intrigue unseated him, and in less than five years he was out of office. Then for thirteen years, from 496 to 483 B. C., he was a wandering teacher, but in the latter year he settled down in his native province, completed his literary work, and in 479 B. C., at the age of seventy-two, he died. He left only one original composition, *Spring and Autumn,* which is said to have had large influence in the reform of the province of Loo.

He died disappointed, and seemed to himself to have been unsuccessful. In his last years he meditated:

"The great mountain must crumble! The strong beam must break! The wise man must wither away like a plant! There is not one in the empire that will make me his master! My time has come to die!"

So it had come, but the whole nation rose up to make him its spiritual master.

There was religion in China before the days of Confucius, but he took little account of it. In some parts of his teachings he implies a belief in deity, as when he says: "The great God has conferred even on inferior people a moral sense, compliance with which would show their nature invariably right." But other of his teachings seem almost to deny the supernatural. He discouraged prayer and did not enjoin any sort of religious observance. He was always modest regarding his own character and attainments, acknowledging four shortcomings, like Buddha, one of which was too much fondness for wine.

WHAT CAN A MAN BELIEVE?

"The Master said: 'In letters I am perhaps equal to other men. But the character of the superior man, carrying out in his conduct what he professes, is what I have not yet attained to.'"

If he fell short of his own ideal, however, he had four great points of strength to which his disciples testified:

"There were four things from which the Master was entirely free. He had no foregone conclusions, no arbitrary premeditations, no obstinacy, no egotism"

He taught the characteristics of the superior man. The ordinary man is partisan and not catholic; the superior man is catholic and not partisan. The superior man does not set himself for or against a given course, but what is right he will do. The superior man is not anxious in the fear of poverty, but is anxious lest he fail to learn the truth.

"In the Book of Poetry are three hundred pieces, but the design of them all can be embraced in one sentence, 'Have no depraved thoughts.'"

He taught the brotherhood of mankind. "Within the four seas all men are brothers." He taught the "silver rule," which is negative as contrasted with the Golden Rule of Jesus, saying, "What you would not have another do to you, do not do to him," but is a noble precept none the less. He taught the value of the family and human nature's unrealized capacities for self-improvement. But his interest was in fitting men for better citizenship, not in the founding of a faith.

It would have amazed him to be told that millions would one day render him worship. Yet for at least twelve hundred years in the temple of Confucius in Pekin the emperor has twice a year offered sacrifice. Twice a year in fifteen hundred and sixty temples similar observances have been carried on for more than a millennium. Less elaborate ceremonies take place twice every month, and no less than sixty-two thousand six hundred and six animals are said to be slaughtered annually in these sacrifices.

"China has produced no other figure who has been so intensely admired. The result of the centuries of devotion paid to him is that the character of the people has been more nearly the creation of this one great teacher than is the case with the people of any other single country in the history of the world."

So says a modern scholar, but the gentle old philosopher himself never dreamed of such immortality. He walked humbly, bemoaning the fact that no one would listen, and regarding his life as a failure; he died worn out and discouraged.

MOHAMMED

There is a legend that a Persian prince once taunted an Arab, saying that his people were inferior to every other race. The Arab demanded, in reply, what nation could be put before the Arabs for strength, beauty, piety, courage, munificence, wisdom, fidelity, pride or hospitality. They only, of the neighbors of the Persians, had maintained their independence. Their fortresses were the backs of their horses. Their beds were the earth. Their roof was the sky. Other nations had need to entrench themselves behind walls of stone and brick, but the Arab trusted in his sword and his courage. Other nations were able to trace their pedigree but a few generations; the Arabs could trace theirs back to Adam, the father of the human race. The Arab was so liberal he would slaughter his camel, his sole wealth, to give a meal to a stranger. No other nation had so elaborate a literature, such noble poetry. Theirs were the finest horses, the most beautiful and most chaste women. No distance was too great for their camels. So sacred was their word that a sign or a look was a binding convenant. So hospitable were they that a guest was protected at the risk of the life of his host. To the Arabs belonged splendid raiment; theirs were mountains filled with gold and silver and gems. Other nations obeyed kings, but they paid no tribute to a central government; every man among them was fit to be a king.

This catalogue of fine qualities is subject to some discount, yet it sets forth the elements of national vitality in which the Arab takes justifiable pride. From such a proud race Mohammed and his religion sprang.

He was born in August 570, a few days after his father's death. His mother died when he was six years old, so that we can not be certain that he ever learned to read and write, though it seems probable that he did. There is, to be sure, a tradition that he wrote the Koran on the breastbones of sheep and as fast as they were filled with words threw them into a chest. The various passages are badly enough arranged to give some substance to the story, but the truth seems to be that the book was really composed and assembled by his followers, and an untidy job they made of it.

WHAT CAN A MAN BELIEVE?

Mohammed's boyhood, like that of the other great religious teachers, is largely hidden from us. We are told that he accompanied his Uncle Zubair on a campaign, carrying arrows for the battle. If this be so, the experience seems to have been of considerable value to him later when he had to engage in fighting on his own account. Somewhere he learned that military success should be followed up promptly, before the defeated foe has opportunity to recover its organization and regain its fighting spirit. And that in battle there is no profit in giving the enemy advantage through a mistaken sense of generosity. These lessons he practised faithfully in his after life.

As manager of a caravan from Mecca to Bostra and back in 594 A. D., he showed some of the qualities essential to success. He took good care of his horses and camels; he had his men under control; he defended his camp against robbers; he was able to dispose of his loads advantageously in Bostra and purchase other cargoes for resale in Mecca. He returned to his home with a profit and increased confidence.

Mohammed was no beauty but he was worth looking at, and his employer, a woman named Khadidjah, a few years older than himself, looked him over thoughtfully. He was of middle height, with black hair, a thick beard, and big, rather clumsy hands and feet. His eyes, which were tinged with red, were large. He was stolidly built, a broad-shouldered man who could be depended upon. He had ability to discern an opportunity and initiative to take advantage of it. Khadidjah decided that he would make a good third husband, and so she married him. Backed by her money, he rose to be a merchant of no mean rank. He continued to travel and trade, his journeys taking him to Syria and Palestine, where he mingled not only with Jews but also with Christians, but for the next ten years we have little record of him.

When he was almost thirty-five he settled a dispute among three sheiks as to how the historic black stone should be replaced in the reconstruction of the Kaaba. The respect with which his decision was received led him to consider his power as a possible teacher of religion. When he was forty he gave his mind to contemplation, and if he were indeed subject to epileptic fits, as has so often been charged, this may have had a share in his supposedly supernatural experiences.

It was in the cave of Hira that he received his call to be a prophet of the one God. He informed his wife of his call, and she believed it to be authentic. Mark this down to Mohammed's credit. If he was self-deceived he was at least sincere enough to make his wife his first convert. She of all people should have known his true spirit. There followed a period of mental depression which has its parallel in the temptations of Jesus and in the heart-searchings of Buddha. But after a time this depression passed, and other revelations followed.

His next two converts were Ali and Zeid, his adopted children. Followed others, until in the sixth year of his prophetic career persecution had begun and some of his followers had fled. On September 2, 622, Mohammed himself fled from Mecca, accompanied by a single companion. After hiding for a time in a cave he came to Medina, where a new epoch in his career begins. The faithful rightly start their calendar with the date of his flight, or Hegira, known in literature as A. H., the year A. D. 622.

During Khadidjah's lifetime Mohammed had no other wife, but within three months after her death he took two wives and thereafter increased the number until he had ten wives and two concubines, a total of thirteen, counting Khadidjah. Khadidjah was the mother of his two sons and four daughters, but neither by her nor any of his other wives did he leave an adult son. His acknowledged descendants, distinguished since 773 A. H. by their green turbans, trace descent from Fatima, daughter of Khadidjah.

As Moslems agree in accepting the date of the Hegira as that which divides the life of Mohammed, so modern commentators, seeking a key to the puzzling tangle of his moral character, have been inclined to go back to the death of Khadidjah as that which changed the peaceable shepherd, camel driver, merchant and teaching prophet into a conquering reformer. What we know is that after he left Mecca he adopted very harsh means for the conversion of those who did not believe. As his following grew, he joined armed attack and plunder with the progress of his cause. One-fifth of all the loot went to him, and in the rest his followers shared alike.

His was a simple doctrine. He denounced infanticide, he opposed strong drink, and he taught the unity of God. The sixfold pledge of Akabah gives his system of morality:

"We will not worship any but the one God. We will not steal. Neither will we commit adultery. We will not kill our children. We will not slander in any wise. Nor will we disobey the prophet in anything that is right."

The doctrine likewise was sixfold:

117

WHAT CAN A MAN BELIEVE?

"Belief in one God; in his Angels; in his Prophets; in the Holy Books, of which the chief and only indispensable one is the Koran; in the Day of Judgment; and in a fatalistic Predestination both of good and evil, so that no man can either hasten or delay his death; 'God wills it' and therefore it is."

Mohammed encouraged rather than forbade polygamy, but limited a man's wives to four, except in his own case. He justified divorce if a man thereby might secure more congenial wives. At one time he tolerated temporary marriage for the convenience of his soldiers in the field, but this did not prove a permanently desirable arrangement and there were usually women captives enough to make it unnecessary.

His conversion was by the sword, and he showed no quarter. He made forays on the neighboring tribes; he made war on Jewish cities; he attacked Christians. And he was successful. There were, indeed, some revolts. Three of his followers set up rival systems, and he fought them. They were not completely subdued at the time of his death but they went under eventually. He brooked no opposition.

Here is a description of him by Kamal ud Din ud Damiri (A. D. 1349-1405):

"Mohammed is the most favored of mankind,

the most honored of all the apostles, the prophet of mercy, the head and commander of the faithful, the bearer of the banner of praise, the intercessor, the holder of high position, the possessor of the River of Paradise, under whose banner the sons of Adam will be on the day of judgment. He is the best of the prophets, and his nation is the best of nations. His companions are the most excellent of mankind, after the prophets, and his creed is the noblest on earth. He performed manifest miracles, and possessed great qualities. He was perfect in intellect, and was of noble origin. He had an absolutely graceful form, complete generosity, perfect bravery, excessive humility, useful knowledge, power of performing high actions, perfect fear of God and sublime piety. He was the most eloquent and the most perfect of manhood in every variety of perfection, and the most distant of men from meanness and vices."

We might doubt his humility, but we have this testimony of Ayesha, his favorite wife:

"The prophet when at home used to serve his own household; he used to pick the vermin from his cloak and patch it, mend his own shoes, and serve himself. He used to give fodder to his camel, sweep the house, tie the camel by the foreleg, eat with the female slave, kneed dough with her, and carry his own purchases from the market."

119

WHAT CAN A MAN BELIEVE?

His tastes were very human. He greatly disliked yellow or decayed teeth and made the use of the tooth-pick almost an article of his religion. He could not endure rank odors; even onion or garlic was offensive to him.

His love for his little girl wife, Ayesha, whom he took at seven and married at ten and who was till death his favorite, becoming an important factor in Moslem politics after his death, shows him at his best. She could do almost anything with him, but she never replaced his loyal memory of Khadidjah.

"Do you not love me more than you loved Khadidjah," she asked him once, "for she was old and unattractive and I am young and beautiful?"

The question was a mistake. He answered with mighty emphasis: "Nay, by Allah! For she it was who first believed in me!"

The prophet was very fond of children, and often stopped to pat their cheeks as he met them on the street. One of his boys died on his breast in the smoky house of his nurse, the blacksmith's wife.

He never cursed. His worst malediction was: "May his forehead be darkened with mud!" When asked to curse some one, he replied: "I have not been sent to curse, but to be a mercy

to mankind." Once, while he was engaged in a
religious conversation with an influential citizen
of Mecca, a blind man drew near and asked him
the way of light and peace. Mohammed turned
away. He never ceased to regret this act. The
surah in the Koran which tells of this incident is
called "He frowned" (Syed, 118). He re-
proached himself that he should have continued
his conversation with the rich when he might
have blessed the poor.

He slept little, being in this respect like
Napoleon, but his extra waking hours were spent
in meditation and worship, for which the pressure of the day left him little time. Yet his
devotions were regular, and he never sat down
to a meal without a blessing or rose without
thanksgiving. Stern as a warrior, and pushing
his victories till they became massacres, there are
yet attributed to him countless deeds of mercy.
He was proud of the fact that when he clasped
a hand he was never the first to withdraw his
palm. He visited often with the sick and whenever he met a funeral procession he turned and
followed it to the grave.

In 631 he issued his famous command that
after four years the Moslems would be absolved
from every league and covenant with idolators.
That was the warning of unrestricted warfare

in the interests of the spread of Islam, and it marked the beginning of the great conquests. But in that same year he had an incurable sorrow. His little son Ibrahim died. He had no male descendant through whom to transmit the scepter of his power. It was the beginning of the end. His warfare had undermined his iron constitution; he was prematurely old, saddened and tired.

From his sick bed he sent out a campaign against the Roman border, and as the troops were departing lifted himself and was taken to the mosque, from whose pulpit he addressed his followers, counseling them to fight bravely and give alms to the poor. Having spoken, he laid his head in the lap of Ayesha and waited for death. He asked for a pitcher of water and, when he had wetted his face, he prayed:

"O Lord, I beseech thee to assist me in the agonies of death." Thrice he prayed, and then at intervals said in a whisper: "Eternity of Paradise! Pardon! Yes, the blessed companionship on high."

Gently he stretched himself and relaxed. His head grew heavy on the breast of Ayesha. The prophet of Arabia was dead. But from ten thousand minarets that stretch from the Atlantic shore across Africa and across Arabia to the

Gulf, his name is recited five times a day, joined
to that of Almighty God:

"There is but one God, and Mohammed is
his prophet."

JESUS

The cathedral of Strassburg, with its spire
four hundred and sixty-five feet high, was one
of the glories of the Middle Ages. One day
when the canons were showing Erasmus through
it, they reminded him proudly that no one could
be admitted to their chapter unless he had at
least fourteen noble ancestors on his father's side
and as many on his mother's. To which their
guest, with characteristic wit, replied: "Then
Christ himself could not have been received into
this chapter unless He got a dispensation from
this rule."

If Buddha would be shocked by the prayer-
wheels of India, grinding out their mechanical
petitions to him; if Confucius would be dis-
mayed by the costly ceremonies and the sacrifice
of animals in his worship, it is likewise true that
Jesus of Nazareth might feel uncomfortable in
some of the temples erected in His name. There
was a very flourishing religion of forms and
ceremonies in Jerusalem when He was born; He
took little interest in it. His message was that

God is a Father who may be approached directly by any of His children, without the mediation of temple or priest. Yet He had hardly gone from the earth before the process began of formalizing this simple doctrine into an imposing structure of cathedrals and creeds.

The story of His life is much more familiar to us than the stories of Buddha, Confucius and Mohammed; hence, we shall treat it rapidly, giving ourselves more space in which to answer the questions: What did He teach? Wherein does His teaching differ from the others? How, if at all, is it better?

The first disciples of Buddha regarded him as a man, but of far nobler quality than themselves. Later disciples made him the son of a god and a virgin, and surrounded his birth with heavenly portents of many sorts. Similarly, the birth of Confucius was said, by later followers, to have been accompanied by supernatural happenings. The four Gospels which record the life of Jesus were written many years after His death: in two of them He is described as the Son of God, born of the Virgin Mary. Belief in His supernatural birth has become a doctrine of the Christian Church, very precious to many of its members.

He grew up in the city of Nazareth and

worked in the carpenter shop of Joseph, His
mother's husband. It is presumed that Joseph
died while Jesus was still a lad, and that He was
responsible for His mother's support until the
younger members of the household were old
enough to take care of themselves. At about the
age of thirty, He laid down His tools and
appeared at the bank of the River Jordan, where
John, a brilliant young cousin, was preaching to
crowds from Jerusalem and the surrounding
territory and signalizing the repentance of converts by baptism in the river. Jesus submitted
Himself for baptism and afterward retired into
the wilderness for a period of self-examination
and prayer.

Returning after forty days, He began to
preach. His first public utterance followed the
pattern of John's, a call for repentance based on
the assurance that the Kingdom of Heaven was
at hand. The two preachers were very dissimilar in taste and temperament. John was
austere and lonely. Jesus was happy by nature,
fond of the companionship of friends. He soon
saw that John's message and methods would not
do for Him. He stayed in the towns or cities, or
walked along the shores of the Lake of Galilee,
surrounded always by a cheerful crowd. Gradually His own message took shape in His mind

and began to have a character quite different from John's.

He told these simple people that God was their Father, and they themselves heirs of immortal life. They heard the news gladly.

"He went about doing good, and healing all oppressed by the devil; for God was with him."

With His increasing popularity His words took on a more authoritative tone. The crowds regarded Him as one who would drive the Romans from Jerusalem and restore the throne of David. The rulers began to take uneasy notice; His close friends were distressed, saying, "He is beside Himself," and fearing that His rash words would involve them all in trouble.

On one occasion His "mother and His brethren" came to interrupt Him in the midst of His teaching and healing, and while the narrative does not explicitly state that their purpose was to restrain Him, scholars have assumed that they too regarded Him as mentally disturbed and were eager to persuade Him to retire from this dangerous enterprise. His reception of their visit indicated that He was well aware of their lack of faith, for He said to those who brought Him the news that they were outside and desired to see Him:

WHICH IS THE BEST RELIGION?

"Who is my mother? and who are my brethren? And he stretched forth his hand toward his disciples, and said, Behold my mother and my brethren! For whosoever shall do the will of my Father which is in heaven, the same is my brother, and sister, and mother."

Herod, the king, had already got rid of John the Baptist by beheading him. That ruthless murder cast a shadow over the life of Jesus, who read in it the prophecy of His own defeat and death. His hopes that the nation might have a spiritual rebirth began to fade. His followers deserted, first a few at a time and then in crowds, until hardly more than his original disciples were left. His latter utterances were often very stern, denouncing the priestly rulers as hypocrites, whited sepulchers and plunderers of the poor. On one of the great feast days, when the city was crowded with pilgrims, He strode into the outer court of the Temple and overthrew the tables of the money changers, released the animals which were there for sacrifice, and cleared the whole court, crying:

"It is written, My house shall be called the house of prayer; but ye have made it a den of thieves."

The high priest, who shared in the profits of the Temple trading, determined that the time had come to put an end to this rebellious young man. Taking Him at night, through the treachery of one of His disciples, they hurried Him through the semblance of a trial in their own courts and brought Him to the Roman governor, Pilate, for permission to put Him to death. This the governor granted reluctantly, and Jesus was crucified, in about the thirty-third year of His age, on a cross between two thieves.

Demoralized by the destruction of their high hopes, His disciples fled into Galilee, hiding themselves in their native villages and returning to their former occupations. The new religion seemed dead. Yet an amazing thing happened. Within a few weeks the disciples were back in Jerusalem, firmly united and fired by a new faith, beginning the crusade which was to carry the name of their Master to the farthest corners of the world. The explanation given by them and recorded in the Gospels is that on the third day after His crucifixion, Jesus arose from the dead, appearing to them on several occasions and instructing them to extend His teaching to all nations.

Contemporary secular records contain no reference to the life of Jesus, His teachings, His crucifixion, or His resurrection. The Gospels, however, have every evidence of historical truth. There can be no reasonable doubt that such a man lived and died, and that those who were closest to Him and in the best position to know were convinced that He rose from the dead—so firmly convinced that they were transformed from beaten, hopeless men into conquering prophets who braved every peril and endured every sort of persecution rather than surrender their faith.

H. G. Wells, in his *Outline of History,* says:

"Yet be it noted that while there was much in the real teachings of Jesus that a rich man or a priest or a trader or an imperial official or any ordinary respectable citizen could not accept without the most revolutionary changes in his way of living, yet there was nothing that a follower of the actual teaching of Gautama Sakya might not receive very readily, nothing to prevent a primitive Buddhist from being also a Nazarene, and nothing to prevent a personal disciple of Jesus from accepting all the recorded teachings of Buddha.

"Again consider the tone of this extract from the writings of a Chinaman, Mo Ti, who lived somewhere in the fourth century B. C., when the doctrines of Confucius and Lao Tze prevailed in China, before the advent of Buddhism to that country, and note how 'Nazarene' it is.

" 'The mutual attacks of state on state; the mutual usurpations of family on family; the mutual robberies of man on man; the want of kindness on the part of the sovereign and of loyalty on the part of the minister; the want of tenderness and filial duty between father and son—these, and such as these, are the things injurious to the empire. All this has arisen from want of mutual love. If but that one virtue could be made universal, the princes loving one another would have no battle-fields; the chiefs of families would attempt no usurpations; men would commit no robberies; rulers and ministers would be gracious and loyal; fathers and sons would be kind and filial; brothers would be harmonious and easily reconciled. Men in general loving one another, the strong would not make prey of the weak; the many would not plunder the few, the rich would not insult the poor, the noble would not be insolent to the mean; and the deceitful would not impose upon the simple.'

"This is extraordinarily like the teaching of Jesus of Nazareth cast into political terms," Mr. Wells continues. "The thoughts of Mo Ti came close to the Kingdom of Heaven. *This essential identity is the most important historical aspect of these great world religions.* They were in their beginnings quite unlike the priest, altar and temple cults, those cults for the worship of definite and finite gods that played so great and so essential a part in the earlier stages of man's spiritual development between 1500 B. C. and 600 B. C. These new world religions, from 600 B. C. onward, were essentially religions of the heart and of the universal sky . . . and it is not to one overcoming the other or to any new variant replacing them that we must look, but to the white truth in each being burnt free from its dross, and becoming manifestly the same truth—namely, that the hearts of men, and therewith all the lives and institutions of men, must be subdued to one common Will, ruling them all."

All four of the great religions agree that the universe is ruled by One Supreme Being, who revealed Himself through the founder of the religion and is further represented by certain sacred scriptures which set forth the way of right living. Mohammed and Confucius wrought no miracles, indeed Mohammed definitely disclaimed miraculous power when challenged to prove his rôle of prophet by exhibiting it. Some of the miracles of Jesus and of Buddha bear a certain resemblance. Thus Jesus walked on the Sea of Galilee and Buddha crossed the River Ganges without a boat. Jesus by a word or the touch of His hand healed the sick; Buddha healed a sick woman by a single look. Jesus fed five thousand on five loaves and two small fishes; Buddha fed five hundred with no previous supplies. Jesus, alone of all the great teachers, is reported to have risen from the dead.

Three of the four great faiths contain the principle of the Golden Rule. Thus Buddha says:

"Is there a deed, Rahula, thou dost wish to

do? Then bethink thee thus: 'Is this deed conducive to my own harm, or to others' harm or to that of both?' Then is this a bad deed, entailing suffering. Such a deed must thou surely not do."

The Silver Rule of Confucius has already been quoted, but since it occurs in six different places in the sacred scriptures of his religion it deserves to be given again:

"The Master replied . . . 'What you do not want done to yourself, do not do unto others.'"

Mohammed, whose doctrine was death to all unbelievers, obviously had no use for such a precept, and both Buddha and Confucius fall far short of the moral majesty of Jesus:

"All things whatsoever ye would that men should do unto you, even so do ye unto them."

And Jesus went even further. He alone of all the great teachers acted uniformly in the spirit of His own precept, even in respect to His enemies, claiming that in so doing He was properly interpreting the character of God:

"I say unto you, Love your enemies, bless them that curse you, . . . That ye may be the children of your Father which is in heaven: for he maketh his sun to rise on the evil and on the good, and sendeth rain on the just and on the unjust."

In what they tell us about the future life the four great religions are widely dissimilar. Mohammed was very specific. His heaven is a garden filled with beautiful women and every sensual delight. To Buddha existence was a sad mixture of sorrow and illusion which no one would wish to have continued, yet most *must* continue through successive eras of penance until final release comes by the blotting out of individual personality. Confucius pictured a shadowy future life, devoid equally of hope or fear and having no relation to the actions or results of the present—a ghostly affair, damp and depressing. The teachings of Jesus were very definite but not detailed. "Where I go," He said, "there ye shall go also." In His Father's house, He said, were many mansions; but He left the picture to be filled in by men's own imaginations, based on the assurance that God is Father and will use His omnipotent power to provide eternal good things for His children.

Thus in the degree and quality of hope and inspiration which they hold out for the future, the four religions are far apart. And each has fixed upon its people the stamp of its own character. The Chinese neither hoping nor fearing, but patiently enduring; the Buddhist renouncing all active effort as useless; the Mohammedan showing no mercy to his foes, already condemned to eternal punishment, but gladly incurring any risk in exchange for the delights of a fleshly heaven; Christianity teaching that every thought and act has eternal significance, that "God is not mocked; for whatsoever a man soweth that shall he reap."

Few will deny that in the face which it turns toward the future Christianity is markedly superior to the other three faiths. And there are three other points of definite superiority.

1. Jesus gave God a nobler character than any of the other teachers. Buddha rather left his followers in doubt as to whether there is a God, and subsequently was deified himself. Confucius speaks sometimes of the "Supreme Ruler," sometimes of "Heaven," but without giving personality to the divine being, certainly without inspiring love. Mohammed's God hardly rises to the height of Jehovah of the Old Testament, a jealous sovereign who fights vigorously on the side of the faithful but decrees merciless death to infidels—a very human God, enjoying the pleasures of appetite and bribing His followers to courage by the promise of

fleshly rewards. Only Jesus spoke of God as a Father, loving all of His children alike, rejoicing in their happiness, sharing their sorrows, seeking patiently and helpfully to redeem them from their sins and prepare them for eternal happiness by the transformation of their spirits into His own perfect character.

2. Jesus alone spoke of Himself as the Son of God, and acted throughout as one who has direct and uninterrupted communication with the Eternal. Neither Confucius nor Buddha talked of God nor evidenced any sense of dependence upon Him. Mohammed's Allah is a decidedly partisan and imperfect Being, short tempered and bitter toward adversaries, but ready at any moment to render a special revelation for the convenience of the prophet in preserving peace in his harem. Even to the gaze of the most critical the life of Jesus is flawless. He lived and talked and died as one conscious at every moment of a divine commission. The soul of man in looking toward Him finds its deepest longings satisfied. If this kindly, happy, friendly man be the Son of God; if God, in His character and actions, is like this, then indeed may one live courageously in the present and hopefully for the future.

3. Christianity alone teaches that the pro-

cess of creation is not finished, that God is not a Creator who, having completed the world, has withdrawn into a secure and distant Heaven, but that He is still immanent, still at work, still available for direct help to all who call on His name. This "Holy Spirit," as Jesus described it, is the divine purpose running through all creation, a "power not ourselves working for righteousness," a force like gravity operating constantly to reenforce all worthy effort and oppose all that makes for wrong. The God of other religions is far off and untroubled by human affairs. The God of Jesus is Father, ever present, ever working, conscious of the fall of a single sparrow, numbering the very hairs of his children's heads, loving them with a love that surpasses human understanding, helping them always to be and do their best.

Thus Christianity is the most optimistic and achieving of all the religions. To what extent the nations that acknowledge it have been made progressive by its spirit and to what degree their own high spirits have entered into it, is a question beyond the depth of this present volume. The United States is Christian and progressive; Mexico is Christian and unprogressive. If Christianity is to have the credit in one instance it can not escape responsibility across the border.

WHICH IS THE BEST RELIGION?

The truth is, of course, that many factors besides religion—climate, blood, diet, inheritance—help to form national character. We are not made by faith alone. Yet Confucianism, with its calm acceptance of things as they are, its lack of interest in the future, has molded China. Buddhism, with its attitude of sad renunciation, is not a faith to spur the spirit. Christianity, whatever its shortcomings, does say constantly to man, "You can do better. The whole world can do better. You can be perfect, even as your Father."

Of all the founders of great religions, Jesus alone died young. Confucius passed out in old age, a sick and disappointed and broken man. Buddha died old, of indigestion. Mohammed passed away in the arms of his favorite wife, old in spirit if not in years. Jesus was cut off in the flower of His youth. He wanted to live. He cried out in agony that the cup of death should be allowed to pass from His lips. He loved life and could look far down the years, seeing many pleasures to enjoy, so much work yet to do.

He spoke with the freshness of firm muscles, sound sleep, low blood pressure, gay sunrises, and deep, strong lungs. There was about Him none of the hesitation of middle life, none of the disillusionment and weakness of age.

The lame could walk, the blind could see, the very dead could rise, if only they believed as He believed.

What middle age and old age might have done to Him we do not know. Fortunately, we do not need even to guess. Those who cut Him off in the full flush of His youth did us an unwitting kindness. They preserved Him for us ever young, full of optimism for the future, full of dissatisfaction with the past. A vigorous, vibrant, joyous Leader, crying: "What I am you can be. What I do you can do, and even greater works. Where I go you can come. All things are possible."

CHAPTER IV

WHAT FEW SIMPLE THINGS CAN A MAN BELIEVE?

WHEN he was a little boy Charles Darwin used to run foot races, and was very often victorious. Years later he wrote this explanation of his youthful assurance: "I prayed earnestly to God to help me, and I well remember that I attributed my success to my prayers and not to my quick running, and marvelled how generally I was aided."

There are many grown-up little boys, beginning now to be gray around the temples, who will read that paragraph with a sympathetic smile. They too remember athletic contests, grammar school examinations, and boyish business ventures in which they were successful because God was on their side. With some feeling of loss and loneliness they look back on those days when there were no doubts, and all life seemed so much simpler.

"I remember, I remember
The house where I was born,
139

WHAT CAN A MAN BELIEVE?

The little window, where the sun
  Came peeping in at morn.

"I remember, I remember
  The fir-trees dark and high;
I used to think their slender tops
  Were close against the sky:
It was a childish ignorance,
  But now 'tis little joy
To know I'm farther off from Heaven
  Than when I was a boy."

To be sure, the God of boyhood was not an altogether comfortable companion. He was stern and busy with bookkeeping. Yet He could be relied upon in an emergency. When a little boy had been good for several days in succession it was possible, by timely prayer, to induce Him to take notice and give real help. That boys should really love Him was almost impossible, however much the Sunday-school teachers might urge it. But the fear of Him was much less dreadful than it had been a few generations before.

Says Harvey J. O'Higgins in his interesting chapter on Julia Ward Howe:

"The training [in her home] was narrow and cloistered and Puritanic to a point that is now almost incredible. Her mother died at the age of twenty-seven, having borne seven children of whom Julia was the eldest living, then five and a half years old. Her mother was 'almost literally prayed to death,' and after her mother's death the father's 'views of religious duty became more stringent' than ever. He read family prayers night and morning. With him Sunday observance began, Puritanically, on Saturday evening. 'The early days of my youth,' she wrote in her *Reminiscences,* 'were passed in the seclusion not only of home life, but of a home most carefully and jealously guarded from all that might be represented in the orthodox trinity of evil, the world, the flesh and the devil.' She was allowed no playmates outside the family connection, and their play was inside play.

"At the age of eight she wrote to a young cousin ill from some childish ailment: 'I hear with regret that you are sick, and it is necessary as ever that you should trust in God; love him, dear Henry, and you will see Death approaching with joy.' At twelve she dedicated a manuscript volume of poems to her father, warning him not to 'expect to find in these juvenile productions the delicacy and grace which pervades the writings of that dear parent who is now in glory.' And the titles of the poems included 'All things shall pass away,' 'We return no more,' 'To an infant's departing spirit,' 'My Heavenly Home,' etc. At fifteen she composed a verse called 'Vain Regrets' with the subtitle 'Written on looking over a diary kept while I was under serious impressions'; and a stanza reads:

" 'Oh! Happy days, gone, never to return
At which fond memory will ever burn,
Oh! Joyous hours, with peace and gladness blest,
When hope and joy dwelt in this careworn
    breast.' "

One would have to think quite a while in order to compose a stanza more foreign to the mind of the modern Christian child. Something must be allowed, of course, for the widely different view-point of that generation, remote from us only a hundred years in time but many centuries remote in its approach to the method and subject-matter of religious instruction. Something must be allowed also for the personality of little Julia Ward Howe. Her over-developed religiosity seems as abnormal to us as some of the sophistication of our children in quite different directions would have seemed to her and her parents. But when all allowances have been made, this stanza and the other poetry in her juvenile book constitute a rather terrible indictment of that type of Christianity which was taught to her. Why should a God-fearing little girl ever have caught up those pious phrases from the lips of older people and made them her own?

Of what use is faith in a loving Father if its effect is to cause sixteen-year-old youngsters to have "careworn breasts"? How could any one imagine that Jesus, the friendliest person who ever lived, whose first miracle was performed to make a happy social party happier, who was followed everywhere by laughing groups of boys and girls, should demand solemn introspection and dyspeptic forebodings as the evidence of belief? By what strange perversion did the laughter and sunshine of His personality become debased into gloom and fear? Surely, these are questions which constitute one of the mysteries of the world.

In your own childhood, gentle reader, religious thinking had considerably improved. Yet there are many people now living who, if they were to make a written inventory of their earliest religious impressions would probably produce a record something like this:

The earth is a testing ground suspended midway between Heaven and Hell. It was thrown together rather impulsively by God in six days. He is an old man with white whiskers, and very vain, since He insists that the principal duty of men and women is to render Him unceasing praise. He placed in the Garden of Eden a most attractive tree as a deliberate temptation to Adam and Eve and, having all knowledge, He was well aware that they would succumb.

When they did, He turned them out of the Garden, sentenced them to labor, pain and sorrow, and condemned their descendants forever. Some generations later, when the human race showed no evidences of perfection, He lost His temper again, repented that He had ever created it, and destroyed practically all life, animal and human, by a world-wide flood. Only Noah and his family were saved, and we are their descendants.

Since the flood the race has been neither better nor worse than before, and practically all of its members were damned until a little over nineteen hundred years ago. At that time Jesus, His only Son, persuaded God to let Him come to earth and die for the human race. By this sacrifice God permitted His wrath to be appeased toward whatever small fraction of humanity should thereafter believe in Jesus and confess His name.

Sunday is God's day, and there must be no pleasure of any sort from morning to night. Religion consists of going to church on Sunday, saying one's prayers at night, and abstaining from wine, women, song and profanity. Hell is a place of eternal torment somewhere under the earth. Heaven is a city beyond the skies, where the streets are paved with gold, and the sole occupation of the inhabitants is playing on harps and telling God how kind and wonderful He is. Many are called but few are chosen and, while one may hope for salvation through a rigid stifling of pleasure and a continuous observance of religious rites, still the chances are against success, and death is a moment of horrible fear. . . .

Overdrawn as this statement may be in parts, it will call up corroborative memories in the minds of many middle-aged readers. The rigid creed with which they started life began to crumble under the influence of high school and college. Astronomy assaulted it. They learned with some dismay that the world is not the center of the universe, supremely important, but merely one tiny speck in a vast collection of worlds. Is it then the only world inhabited by intelligent beings? Would God build so great a universe and let so much go to waste—a hotel of a million rooms in which only one was tenanted? It does not sound reasonable. But if there are other worlds, inhabited by beings like ourselves or better, must not these inhabitants also be children of God? And, if so, had Jesus descended upon these other worlds to die, repeating indefinitely the tragic drama of His earthly experience?

Biology and history delivered other blows.

145

They showed no record of Adam and Eve, beings created perfect and fallen by sin to a lower plane. On the contrary, they pictured a slow, painful struggle upward, a "survival of the fittest"—progress achieved by bitter epochs of selection but resulting always in something better. If their records were true; if there had been no fall through Adam, then what became of the frightful wrath of the Creator and the appeasing atonement of the Son?

The process of disillusionment was bewildering. Millions of earnest, sincere people were shaken, and knew not what to believe. They echoed the protest of the historian Froude, who said: "If medicine had been regulated three hundred years ago by Act of Parliament; if there had been Thirty-nine Articles of Physic, and every practitioner had been compelled under pains and penalties to compound his drugs by the prescriptions of Henry the Eighth's physician, Doctor Butts, it is easy to conjecture in what state of health the people of this country would at present be found."

Medicine has constantly progressed by rejecting the old truth for the new; science rejects and moves forward; business refuses to regard precedent as binding or even, in many instances, instructive. To many modern-minded folk, accustomed to almost daily revisions of their thinking in every other department of life, it seemed that religion alone was unprogressive, still clinging stubbornly to the "faith once delivered to the saints." From this old fixed faith their progressive intelligence turned away, and great groups of them assumed that there was nothing to be set up in its place. So it happened that religion, which if it be true should be as natural a part of human experience as eating or talking or moving, dropped out of the daily thinking of many upright and kindly people.

Josh Billings years ago uttered the warning that the man who can not talk with you five minutes without speaking about his soul "will bear the closest kind of watching." Most of us share that prejudice. We shy off from notoriously religious folk, and are unspokenly suspicious of those who have no redeeming vices. If a newspaper sends us a questionnaire asking, "Do you believe in God?" we write a weak "yes" in lead pencil and mail it back anonymously. But men may live for years together in business or social relationships without discovering the slightest evidence of each other's religious views.

Everything else, including subjects that once were kept behind the veil, we discuss with quite appalling frankness. We chatter about the theater for hours, but about the eternal drama, or tragedy, of man's creation, preservation and ultimate fate, never a word. We see our friends off for California and follow them enviously in our imaginations and conversations; we see our friends off on the Great Journey and come away with bent heads and sealed lips, not quite daring to say boldly, "I believe."

It may almost be said that to talk about religion is no longer good form. That snobbish lady, Convention, whose nod is stronger than a constitutional amendment, has pronounced the subject old-fashioned. Even some preachers go about as if their success depended on having men forget that they are preachers. They organize clubs, attend ball games, and are good fellows generally, but their entrance into a group of men brings no consciousness that a prophet has entered, in whom are the words of eternal life. A great conspiracy of silence! Yet secretly, furtively, deep down, there is hardly a thinking man who does not cling to some remnant of belief; even an Ingersoll at his brother's grave cries out: "From the voiceless lips of the unreplying dead there comes no word; but in the night of death hope sees a star and listening love can hear the rustle of a wing."

WHAT FEW SIMPLE THINGS?

In these pages it is our purpose to take religion out of the hush-hush category. We contend
that the present situation is cowardly and absurd. Either faith is something or it is nothing.
If it be nothing; if, because of the newer
revelations of science, there be left no foundation
for belief which an intelligent man can accept
and build on, then the quicker we admit that fact
and have done with it the greater our self-respect. If we are only animals, created out of the
dust for no purpose and doomed to destruction,
let us say so frankly, dismiss hope from our
thoughts, and go forward as courageously as we
can.

> "We are but fellow travellers
> Along life's dusty way;
> If any man can play the pipes,
> In God's name, let him play."

If, however, there be a real solid basis, however simple, for religious faith, then we add
greatly to our own courage and that of our
comrades if we examine it, accept it, and treat
it as a frank and normal part of human experience. The middle ground of half-ashamed
silence is unworthy. As long as we occupy it we
are like locomotives on dead center, without
movement of our own and useless as movers of
others.

WHAT CAN A MAN BELIEVE?

Theology begins with creeds, and most of the creeds are old and were written by men whose knowledge of the world was very limited. Any high-school boy could pass a better examination in geography than St. Augustine; even a college sophomore knows more than the popes of a century ago. Spiritually these ancients were giants who towered high and believed, at least, that they talked with God. But in this present chapter we dismiss both them and their creeds; we are not going to be guided to Heaven by men who supposed that the earth was flat. Nor will we submit to theology's demand that we start by a great act of faith. Theology always starts that way. "I believe in God, the Father Almighty," it says, and insists that all men repeat this tremendous assumption.

We will not be commanded. It is not our business habit to begin our thinking with what is farthest off and most difficult to prove. We start with what we know. That is the way business is built up. It is the way scientific knowledge grows.

If engineers were given the task of surveying a small inland lake, they would either drag their chains along the shore or wait until the water was frozen and measure the margin on the ice, setting up their compass at each angle and making an accurate plat. But if the job were much bigger, say a survey of Chesapeake Bay, for example, a different method would have to be pursued. In such a case they would select a level stretch of shore for a base line, and the distance between the two terminal points would be measured again and again to secure the greatest possible accuracy.

From each end of that base a line would be sighted to a conspicuous point on the opposite shore, and the angles carefully measured. With one side and two angles known, the other angle and the other two sides of the triangle could be determined by mathematics. There then would be three base lines, two of them extending across the bay, and these could be used for other measurements. It might be that the whole of Chesapeake Bay could be thus surveyed and only one base line actually measured with the chain. But that line would be one that could actually be walked over and its length determined to a microscopic fraction of an inch. Any error in that first measurement would repeat itself and perhaps multiply itself in all the subsequent computations. The base line *must* be at this end.

By a similar process astronomers measure the distance to the stars. At six o'clock in the evening observation may be taken upon the moon, or one of the planets in the solar system. At six o'clock in the morning the earth will have turned half-way around, and the observer may take a second observation with two angles and a base line of eight thousand miles, being the diameter of the earth. In six months the earth will have traveled half-way around its orbit, giving a base line of one hundred and eighty-six million miles, and with that very respectable distances may be computed. But no astronomer begins by assuming the distance from the North Star to the Pleiades and endeavoring therefrom to compute the earth's diameter or its distance from the moon. He begins with what can be measured and weighed and known. Theology begins with God, the unknowable; science begins at this end.

Curiously enough Jesus began at this end also. As Harry Emerson Fosdick has pointed out in a recent book, it was not the teaching of Jesus about God which got Him into trouble with the authorities. The Pharisees believed in God devoutly. He might have gone on forever saying that God is loving, that He sends rain on the just and on the unjust, and so forth, without exciting the least opposition. It was His teaching about man that stirred up the vested interests. When He said that the prodigal son was entitled to as much of the fatted calf as the home-staying, holier-than-thou brother; when He held up a Samaritan as being more truly religious than a priest; when He said that harlots and publicans would go into the Kingdom of Heaven ahead of the self-seeking, greedy and oppressive (but very pious) Pharisees—these were the speeches for which they crucified Him.

And His teaching was this: If you love your brother you love God. If you say you love God and hate your brother you are a liar. In other words, the way to know God is not to think too much about Him, certainly not to argue about Him, but to know and love your brother. If you give anybody a cup of cold water you are giving it to God. If you forgive your enemies you are acting like God. If you, being evil, know how to give good gifts to your children, you can get some idea of the way in which God, who is not evil nor limited by human weakness, is going to give good gifts to you.

"If you would see his monument," says the epitaph of the great architect, Sir Christopher Wren, in the wall of St. Paul's Cathedral, "look about you." So Jesus said: "If you would see God look about you. He is in your brother, your sister, your parents, your business associates." The creed of Jesus, if He had a creed, began at this end.

Beginning then at this end, what is the

simplest, most certain thing that we can write down? It is this:

1. I believe in myself.

Some philosophers have not accepted even that. They have been full of tortuous subtleties to prove that no man really knows whether he is or isn't; that all outward things exist merely as mental images, and that you and I are only figments of our own imaginations. In this book we consign such philosophers—not the *real* ones, but the imitations—to the ash can. For five thousand years, more or less, they have been sitting in tight rooms, consuming their own carbon dioxide, and the net result of it all, so far as the average man is concerned, is nothing but haze and confusion.

I know that I am. The most important discovery I ever made was that when I got my toe into my mouth it was not quite the same as when I got a corner of the blanket of my crib into my mouth. I discovered that my toe was the limit, in that direction, of the thing I was beginning to think of as me. When I got my toe into my mouth, my mouth gave a feeling of satisfaction and so did the toe. With the blanket it was different. There was a great division in the universe; there was Me, and the things outside Me.

A little later I made a second discovery. If I

cried hard enough my mother would come to me, but the moon and the ceiling would not. So there was another division in the universe: the things I could influence by crying for them, and the things that would not be moved by my tears. In other words, the things like me—my mother, my father, my sisters and brothers, and other folks—and the things unlike me—walls, ceilings, suns, moons, trees. To both those kinds of things I sustained certain relations, as I very early learned; for example, it made a difference whether I fell out of bed into my mother's arms or whether I fell out on to the floor.

There were three ways in which I assured myself of myself. The first was my knowledge that when a pin stuck into me I was much less happy than when I had had my dinner and was almost asleep. That is to say, I knew the difference between pleasure and pain; I could feel. The next was when I knew what I wanted and tried to get it in the only way I had mastered, by crying for it. That is to say, I had the power of will. Last of all, I began to think. I have kept at all three of these processes more or less ever since. And no philosopher can talk me out of the first article of my creed. *I know that I am.*

2. I know that I am intelligent. This is the second article.

I can plan as well as think. I can lay out a

program covering a week, a month, a year, five years, and go through with it, foreseeing difficulties and making provision for the unexpected. Given a certain result, I can reason back to the causes; and vice versa, being provided with the elements of a problem, I can formulate them into an answer.

I know that my intelligence (and by *me* I mean, of course, mankind) is the highest and most powerful thing in the natural universe. Nature is subject to it, for I can harness the winds and the water-falls, remove mountains and cause rivers to turn back on their courses. All animals are subject to it, for I can outthink and outplan them. They have a wide range of emotions; they fear, hate, love, sorrow, perhaps they dream. But I alone stand erect, looking back as well as forward, capitalizing experience, predicating the future on my memory of the past, seeing for myself, in imagination, a more favorable set of circumstances and proceeding by my own will to make my dreams come true.

I have intelligence.

3. Thus far there is nothing in my creed which even the most critical modern man would not accept. A bank president would okeh it; a chartered accountant would certify it; an income tax collector would, perhaps re-

luctantly, say that it is all right. Comes now the only step which requires imagination. Comes now an act of faith.

Because I have intelligence, there must be Intelligence behind the universe. Let us venture to repeat that. Because I have intelligence there must be Intelligence behind the universe. Why? Because otherwise the universe has created something greater than itself, for it has created me; and the assumption that the lesser can produce the greater, that something can come out of nothing, does violence to my common sense. I can not conceive or accept it. In other words, because I am, I believe God is.

It has been said that no astronomer can be an atheist; that no man who spends his nights looking through a telescope, who sees the marvelous balance and rhythm of the planets and the stars, who learns that even the comets, those seemingly lawless and irresponsible members of the firmament, perform according to a schedule so that their reappearances can be predicted accurately years in advance; that no man who delves into the mysteries of this ordered and law-abiding universe can convince himself that its performance is merely a matter of chance. The deeper his researches the more profound his faith!

WHAT CAN A MAN BELIEVE?

There was a gentleman named Paley whose name has come down to us in connection with a famous argument about a watch. Summarized rather freely, the good Doctor's argument was something like this: "In crossing a heath one day I strike my toe against a watch. I pick it up and note that it consists of a complicated arrangement of wheels, springs, jewels, and balances, all neatly combined in a case and covered with a crystal. On closer examination I discover that every tiny piece of its intricate mechanism is performing according to a definite schedule, and each part is so related to the others that the hands are moved about the dial according to a dependable and unvarying routine. Having never seen a watch made, I conclude that this watch had no maker; that out of the bowels of the earth came iron and gold, and the elements of glass; that they refined themselves, fashioned themselves into springs and wheels and crystal, assembled themselves into this case, wound themselves up and started to tick. I show you the watch and tell you my story," said Paley, "and you tell me I am a fool. You say that my story violates your reason; that the existence of the watch is positive evidence of the pre-existence of a watch-maker.

"And yet," he continues, after many pages—

and we are still paraphrasing freely—"and yet I show you a far more tremendous mechanism, a watch whose parts are planets and stars, suspended in limitless space, moving in unvarying orbits, each perfectly adjusted to all the others and so cunningly contrived that tides are made to rise and fall, seasons to rotate, crops to appear in summer, and snow to cover the earth in winter as a preparation for further crops—I show you all this, and you say: 'It is a mystery beyond our understanding. It must have happened. There is no evidence of an Intelligence; no proof of a Plan.'"

Paley's watch is not cited so frequently as it used to be. The statement that "no astronomer can be an atheist" is an argument and not a proof, yet I find it convincing in those months which I spend in the country where one can look up and see the stars. In the city where I make my own stars by touching a button, where I control heat and cold by the turn of a valve and order my existence by the touch of a toe on the throttle of a car or a scratch on the bottom of a check—in the city and the winter the stars do not speak so loudly.

I fall back then upon my own self-knowledge. I say: Since no one can prove either that there is a God or that there is not, each one of us has a right to accept the alternative which does least violence to his own reason. To my finite mind God is inconceivable, but a universe which just happened is *more* inconceivable. A Divine Intelligence is beyond my meager comprehension, and as for the Divine Plan, I do not see what it is; but I know that men and women are intelligent, and to believe that an unintelligent universe has produced something greater than itself; that molecules of matter, combining through the ages, have evolved into the mind that wrote Shakespeare's sonnets, or fashioned the statues of Phidias, or composed Mozart's Minuet, or led Jesus of Nazareth to die on the cross rather than compromise—this to me is absurdity. I can not accept it. It is far easier, far more reasonable to believe that all intelligence is somehow a part of a Great Intelligence; that because I think, God thinks, because I plan, He plans.

4. Since, then, there is a God, what kind of a God is He?

My answer is that He must be at least as good as I am, for He created me, and my intelligence is a tiny fragment of His own. And I know in my heart that I am much better than most of the mental images which men have created in the past and labeled with the name of "gods." (The philosophers point out to us, of course, that all gods have been created in the image of the men who worshiped them. Thus Spinoza says: "I believe that a triangle if it could speak would say that God is eminently triangular, and a circle that the divine nature is eminently circular; and thus would every one ascribe his own attributes to God!") I do not hesitate to ascribe my own best attributes to God, and I should be willing to take my chance in a universe ruled by One whose worst nature is as good as my best. So would you; so would any man.

For what sort of people are we, at our best? We do not like to see others suffer. We do not punish children for mistakes which they make unwittingly; we should not sentence a mad dog or a rattlesnake to eternal torture. It gives us pleasure to see men and women happy, and if we had unlimited wealth and power nothing would please us more than the fun of sharing liberally with the weak and poor. We bring children into the world knowing that by that act we increase our own burdens, tie ourselves to hard work for life, add to our responsibilities and cares and, to that extent, limit our happiness. Yet in nothing do we feel ourselves so ennobled as in parenthood. We "give until it hurts"; we utterly cast aside any thought of our own pleasure in our consuming desire for our daughters and sons; we even, under splendid need, "lay down our lives for our friends." This is the kind of people we are when we are at our best. Surely, God is no worse.

With such a God there must, it seems to me, be some sort of life beyond the grave. I believe this, not because I particularly crave it; sometimes, indeed, when I am thoroughly tired out, it seems as if an eternity of rest would be more desirable than an eternity of life. But when I am at the top of my game, then it is that I have the craving to go on—and so do you. So does everybody. And to my way of thinking immortality of some sort is a necessary complement to the existence and nature of God.

For why was the universe set going in the first place? To what end is all the struggle and suffering and self-sacrifice? To produce a nobler race, a finer character? And for what? To blot it all out in the end? Where is the justice in such a plan? Would you, if you were God, create in man the conviction that life is significant, that there is an eternal difference between right and wrong, that love and self-sacrifice and devotion and loyalty are important—would you make them feel all this, and act in accordance with it, often to their own hurt, and then laugh at them in the end? You would not.

I can not picture Heaven. My former ideas are all unsatisfying, and I have no new ideas to fill their place. I have ceased to try to picture it. But there must be some place hereafter where life goes on, where injustices are righted and inequalities evened up, where those who have been thwarted and disappointed and cheated are given a fairer field and a better chance. This world as we know it can not be the whole answer, for it does not square with intelligence. And Intelligence is God.

The fact that I can not construct in my imagination a hereafter which is anything less than eternal boredom does not worry me a particle. Every day I am made to realize anew that what I call my mind is a very elementary organ, and that already science has leaped into mysteries which are completely beyond its grasp. I turn the knob of my radio, and music comes to me out of the air. I do not understand it; I never shall. I read in the paper a speech by a man named Einstein who says that there is no such thing as time or space. It merely makes my poor brain stagger, yet I know that to abler brains than mine it means something, though even they admit that they have only begun to begin to understand. I comfort myself with the remark of William James, who said:

"I firmly disbelieve, myself, that our human experience is the highest form of experience extant in the universe. I believe rather that we stand in much the same relation to the whole universe as our canine and feline pets do to the whole of human life. They inhabit our drawing rooms and libraries. They take part in scenes of whose significance they have no inkling. They are merely tangent to curves of history, the beginnings and ends and forms of which pass wholly beyond their ken. So we are tangent to the wider life of things."

That makes sound sense to me. A God with imagination enough to create oceans, and solar systems and sexes, and seasons and poets, and mountains and mothers and martyrs—such a God can be trusted to make the hereafter just and satisfying and full of interest. I think about it very little, but I shed few tears at funerals. I leave it all to Him.

This seems to me a minimum creed, a few stones laid solid on which a man may rest his feet. It leaves much to be explained. A great scientist remarked that whatever one may believe about the future of God, no man of feeling can forgive His past; by which he meant the bloody path of suffering which we call "evolution."

Why should a loving God have chosen such a cruel process by which to bring creation up to higher levels? Why the heartless struggle for existence; the slaughter of millions for the survival of one? Why does all life prey upon itself, the larger devouring the lesser, and being devoured in turn? Why suffering? Why pain? Why the blasting of hopes, the striking down of righteousness by ill health and trials undeserved? Why do the wicked flourish like the green bay tree? What substantial basis is there for the faith of a man

"Who trusts that God is love indeed,
     And love creation's final law;
Though nature, red in tooth and claw,
     With ravin shrieks against the creed."

Where in all the horrible destructiveness of nature does one look for evidence of design and proof of love?

To these questions my simple creed gives no clear answer. Nor does it deal at all with those theological doctrines around which most of the great battles of Christian history have been waged. In a later chapter we shall have something to say about Jesus, and the church, and of the forms in which the faith of the future may conceivably express itself. But for the present we rest upon these few fundamentals: We believe in ourselves. We know that we are intelligent, therefore we believe that there is Intelligence behind the universe, for to assume that the universe could produce something greater than itself does violence to our common sense. We believe that this Intelligence is good, because we ourselves are good. We know that it plans because we plan; we are content to trust in its planning and to assume that somehow, behind the seeming cruelties and inconsistencies, there is a purpose to which all things are clear.

Two things are worth saying in conclusion. The first is that the old-time "conflict between science and religion" is dead. As a matter of fact, there never was any conflict between science and religion, only between science and theology. Theology is to religion what botany is to flowers. One may love roses and know nothing of botany; one may have faith and know nothing of creeds. Modern religion is scientific in its attitude of eager searching, in its prayer: "Oh, God, give us more and more truth, for we know that Thy revelation of Thyself was not completed and closed in the distant past but continues and will always continue." And modern science is religious in its frank confession that beyond its farthest reaches there is the vast Unknowable, and its humble confession that each day's knowledge needs revising in the light of each new sun.

"How little we know about the ultimate nature of things is strikingly shown by the changes in our conceptions which have come within the past thirty years," said that great physicist and Nobel Prize winner, Dr. Robert Andrews Millikan, in *Collier's Weekly* some months ago. "When I started my graduate work in 1893 we were very sure that the physical foundations of the world were built with some seventy unchangeable, indestructible elements.

"Also we made a sharp distinction between matter-physics and ether-physics. We believed in the conservation of energy, the conservation of mass, and the conservation of momentum, and we knew exactly how, with the aid of these principles, the universe managed to keep going. But we are much less certain about this now than we were then.

"In 1895 the X-ray came in as an absolutely new phenomenon, and then came radio-activity, which has shown us that 'the elements' are not at all ultimate things, that atoms are continually undergoing change, and are not indestructible. It appears now that the electro-magnetic laws no longer hold in the interaction of electrons within atoms. Einstein has concluded that mass and energy are interchangeable terms and we all now agree that the former distinctions between material, electrical and ethereal phenomena must be discarded. . . .

"We firmly believed for many years that the sun was merely a white-hot body gradually cooling off. Now we know that if it were merely that it would have cooled off long ago, and we are searching for the source of its continuous supply of heat and are inclined to the belief that it is due to some form of sub-atomic change. Our discoveries in this realm are as revolutionary as were those of Copernicus but no one thinks of them as anti-religious.

"The impossibility of real science and real religion ever conflicting becomes evident when one examines the purpose of science and the purpose of religion. The purpose of science is to develop without prejudice or preconception of any kind a knowledge of the facts, the laws and the processes of nature. The even more important task of religion, on the other hand, is to develop the consciences, the ideals, and the aspirations of mankind.

"Many of our great scientists have actually been men of profound religious convictions and life. Lord Kelvin's estimate of the age of the earth at around a hundred million years did not seem to him or to the church to be in conflict with the first chapters of Genesis. He said:

" 'I believe that the more thoroughly science is studied the further does it take us from anything comparable to atheism.' And again: 'If you think strongly enough you will be forced by science to the belief in God, which is the foundation of all religion. You will find it not antagonistic but helpful to religion.'

"Take other great scientific leaders—Sir Isaac Newton, Michael Faraday, James Clerk-Maxwell, Louis Pasteur. All these men were not only religious men but they were also faithful members of their communions. For the most important thing in the world is a belief in moral and spiritual values—a belief that there is a significance and a meaning to existence—a belief that we are going somewhere! These men could scarcely have been so great had they been lacking in this belief.

"And it is because of this belief that men are willing to work and to die for causes. Men and women prefer to die rather than to live in the consciousness of having played the coward, of having failed to play their part worthily in the great scheme of things. It is true that not all men are like that, but I am optimist enough to think that most men are. Why? Simply because most men believe that there is a world scheme, that they are a part of it, that their deaths are going to contribute to its development; in short, because most men believe in God."

When the greatest minds in modern science hold such belief, how silly it is for any man to fear that his intelligence is belittled by the act of faith. Not big minds but little minds are cynical. Those who think that science has destroyed religion get their science from the Sunday supplements. The great scientists exercise their souls by wonder, fill their spiritual lungs with the atmosphere of awe, and make their new discoveries on their knees. This is the first thing worth remembering.

And the second is akin to it, and is this: the ablest men in all walks of modern life are men of faith. Most of them have much more faith than they themselves realize. Ask them if they are religious, and they may hesitate to answer yes. Seek to talk to them about religion, and they may draw into their shells. They think that they have no creed, yet hardly one of them would deny the simple, common-sense argument set down in this chapter. And it is a creed; it is religious.

They are great human beings, these modern business men. So determined to stand straight that they lean over backward; so eager to state no more than the truth that they often stop at much less. There was one of their sort in the life of Jesus, a captain in the Roman army, a successful administrator and a rich man. He sent to Jesus and asked for the healing of his servant. The disciples and other Jewish friends

in Capernaum carried the message apologetically. They said in effect: "This man is a
pagan, Lord. He is a kind and generous man, a
contributor to our churches and we wish you
would do something for him if you can. But, of
course, he is lacking in faith."

That was the man's own estimate of himself,
as well. He would have called himself a good
citizen, a supporter of all worthy causes, but religious? No. Yet of that man Jesus said: "I
have not found so great faith, no not in Israel."

The men who are building great businesses,
who are laying large plans which they know can
not be fulfilled in their own lifetimes, who are
planting this year the seeds that will not ripen
for a generation, who are giving freely of themselves for every helpful project—these are the
men who sometimes say: "Of course, I am not
religious"; who maybe feel uncomfortable if
religion is brought into the talk. Yet their whole
lives are tremendous experiments in faith, and
deep down inside them are voices that will not
be stilled. It was men like them, and not priests
or professional philanthropists, whose companionship Jesus chose. It was to one of them that
He remarked: "I have found nowhere such
faith."

The plea of this book is for a frank recognition of the truth that the faith which begets great achievement and the faith which worships are both of the same spirit; that religion is as natural and normal a part of human experience as birth and growth and hope and love. We say it is time to take religion out of the hush-hush class; to recognize frankly and normally that every worth-while enterprise is an act of faith, that

> "There is no unbelief;
> Whoever plants a seed beneath the sod
> And waits to see it push away the clod,
> He trusts in God."

CHAPTER V

Two literary productions have recently appeared in which preachers have leading parts. One is *Abie's Irish Rose,* a drama condemned by the critics but supported more liberally by the public than any play ever produced. The other is *Elmer Gantry,* a novel by Sinclair Lewis, condemned by the critics and by a large majority of readers yet selling more copies than any novel of the year.

In the play a young man, who is a Jew, and a girl, who is an Irish Catholic, are married by a Methodist preacher. The preacher does not appear on the stage, but a Jewish rabbi and a Catholic priest are shown; and these men, being neither ultra-holy nor blessed with supernatural ability, are sensible men, each loyal to his own faith and tolerant of the faith of others, each interested in helping to restrain bigotry and in making life better for everybody.

The book presents as its principal character

173

a loud-mouthed, ignorant exhorter, drunken, loose in his relations with women, adept in the practise of church politics, vulgar and insincere. Borne on the high wave of his own physical vitality, and propelled by his own strong lungs, he rises triumphant over moral disasters that would have sunk other men, and passes out of our sight as the popular pastor of a big city church. This book, advertised in advance by the publishers as "Lewis' great preacher novel," invites the inference that Rev. Elmer Gantry is a representative pastor, typical of the thousands of clergymen who are the responsible leaders of American church life to-day.

It happens that I know a good deal about ministers. They came to my boyhood home in considerable numbers. Perhaps I have seen more than my share of the seamy side of ministerial life. Preachers who were having trouble with their churches came to consult my father. Preachers out of a job came to ask his help—and there are few men more forlorn than a preacher out of a job. Often these men stayed for meals with us and talked over their troubles at the table. None of them was a great man. Many of them reminded me of the old saying of Governor Ford of Illinois, who remarked that while nearly all the early preachers of that state were without higher education, they, nevertheless, ignorant as they were, had no difficulty in finding congregations still more ignorant.

As one of his official duties my father was for many years chairman of a body that had to do with ministerial standing. It was his duty to investigate irregularities of ordination, fraudulent certificates of licensure, and the records of men who had split churches in one denomination and were trying to slip across the line into the ranks of another. Cases of ministerial immorality came before him, and more than once he had the sad task of unfrocking a bad preacher. I heard him one day address a group of young men who were just being commissioned for the ministry. He said in effect:

"By what this council is about to do to you it is vastly increasing your power for harm. Yesterday, as laymen, you might have committed any possible sin and been sent to jail for it, and not much attention would have been paid to you. But to-morrow any one of you can get his name on to the front pages of every paper in the United States. Not many of you have ability or piety enough to achieve high distinction, or to bring the church great honor, but the least conspicuous of you for ability can bring the whole church into shame."

WHAT CAN A MAN BELIEVE?

I can remember a night when he came home tired and depressed after carrying out the sentence of the church upon some miserable offender, and how my sister exclaimed: "Mother, I do wish that father would get off that firing committee."

All in all, I could produce a considerable collection of material for an essay on the sins of preachers.

Yet the truth is that this material would represent no larger a fraction of my total memories of preachers than the percentage of impurity in Ivory Soap. The great bulk of my memories is all on the other side. The thing that stands out most clearly in my childish pictures of those visiting men of God is their fund of funny stories, and the laughter that used to rock our little frame house when they gathered around the table. They were hearty eaters, good jokers, and their laughter was noisy and contagious. They were, of course, all poor, and often their hair needed cutting and frequently they tended to be shiny about the seams. Yet I can hardly recall ever hearing money mentioned. The talk was rather of books, and of church methods, and of people who needed help more than themselves.

I knew quite intimately the details of one

ministerial budget and of how many young people it sent through college, and how many destitute families it held together, and how many thousands—literally thousands—of times it gave help in critical hours of human distress. I once thumbed through the check-book of a preacher's wife, noting from the stubs where her little income had gone. No one could have finished it dry eyed.

The first important magazine assignment ever given to me was to write a series of articles exposing Billy Sunday. I was young and full of crusader enthusiasm. It was in the days when a man could most easily make a magazine reputation by muck-raking, and I started out with the full intention of becoming a national figure overnight. The editor who commissioned me was a man of sincere purpose. He believed thoroughly that Billy Sunday was out only for the money and that the quicker he was exposed the less harm he would do to the church. Our plan was to make an intensive study of three towns: one where he had been three years previously, one where he had been two years previously, and one where his visit was just a year old. We expected to find that his converts had all backslidden, that the churches were worse off than before he came, and that there was no permanent record of his campaign except the sore spot in the town's pocketbook.

In this spirit I set out.

And what I discovered amazed me. In each town, two of which were cities of between thirty and forty thousand people and the third was a country village, I took the list of his converts and checked it up against the church membership rolls. I found, of course, that many converts had slipped away, but in every church a large proportion of the strongest members were men who had come in under his influence. I talked to the merchants, and they told me that during the meetings and afterward people walked up to the counter and paid bills which were so old that they had long since been written off the books.

The president of the chamber of commerce, in the town Billy had visited three years before me, summed up the general opinion. "I am not a member of any church," he said. "I never attend. But I'll tell you one thing. If it was proposed now to bring Billy Sunday to this town, and if we knew as much about the results of his work in advance as we know now, and if the churches wouldn't raise the necessary funds to bring him, I could raise the money in half a day from men who never go to church. He took eleven thousand dollars out of here, but a circus comes here and takes out that amount in one day and leaves nothing. He left a different moral atmosphere."

Rather apologetically I went back to the editor and told him that, while there were lots of things in Billy's work to criticize—and we did criticize them—we should have to write a very different series of articles than we had intended.

I believe that a similar investigation into the work of nine preachers out of ten, anywhere in the United States, would yield similar results. It would show instances of pettiness and failure, to be sure, but it would reveal an amount of self-sacrifice and kindliness and sincere struggle to be worthy such as no one can possibly imagine unless he has had the privilege—and perhaps I ought to say also the pain—of growing up in a parsonage.

So at the outset of this chapter I wish to pay tribute to clergymen of all denominations— Protestants, Catholics and Jews. The experiences of the past two years have given me an added opportunity to learn something about their fine spirit and generous courtesy. Nothing was further from my thought five years ago than that I should be the author of a religious book, to say nothing of a series of such books. The idea that resulted in *The Man Nobody Knows* had been in my mind for a long time. I waited in the hope that somebody better qualified than I would set it forth and when, at length, I sat down to write it I was full of misgivings. Friends warned me that I should be scoffed at by the unbelieving and crucified by the righteous. The preachers particularly would have me in derision.

What happened? An occasional preacher did denounce, and doubtless many who said nothing were offended but suffered their hurt in silence. Here and there a church paper spoke harshly. But all this was a minority expression. The majority vote was amazing. An English lord wrote that the book had been recommended to him by an Anglican bishop. Thousands of sermons have been preached about it all over the English-speaking world, and probably ten thousand pastors have used it in their Bible classes.

A Catholic priest in New England chided me gently for my theological shortcomings. I replied:

"Dear Father:
"I appreciate the tone and spirit of your note and thank you for it. But what is the use of you and me debating about theology, on which we shall never agree? What I should like to learn from you, as a priest of the Infallible Church, is

this: Will there be any good eighteen hole golf courses in Heaven?"

To which, after a few days, the good father answered:

"My Son:
"I think there will be, and I shall meet you there."

If I or any other layman had undertaken to write a book on medicine or law, is it likely that either the doctors or the lawyers would have dealt with it so gently? I doubt it. But the clergymen have been generous to a fault. Their attitude has a twofold significance. It is a fine testimony to their spirit of tolerance and fair play, and for this I shall be grateful as long as I live. But the fact that they should welcome so warmly such a book from one entirely outside the professional pale suggests that they are not comfortable in the present situation. They have a consciousness that the church is in possession of tremendous opportunities on which it is not realizing fully: they are almost too eagerly reaching for help from any honest source.

What will appear in the following pages is heresy of the first order. It will run contrary to the orthodox convictions and prejudices of all

181

sorts of people. Yet I hope it will stimulate honest thinking, even audacious thinking; the situation seems to demand thinking of that type. From those who are going to disagree with it I ask only an acceptance of what I hope will be evident in every line—that it is written in no spirit of destructive criticism but with a genuine desire to help.

When we survey the religious situation in the United States to-day, what do we find?

The Catholic Church, on the whole, is doing its task successfully. Whether or not its organization, doctrine and ritual correctly interpret the ideas of Jesus of Nazareth, the great fact remains that it keeps its hold on the hearts of its people, that to many, many millions it stands for comfort and faith and the hope of eternal life. No man of reverent spirit can pass its altars without bowing his head; and it is hard to understand how any good citizen can doubt that, with all its intolerance and the frequently mistaken ambitions and worldly interests of its leaders, it is a power for righteousness and good.

The Protestant Church presents a confused and baffling picture. In some suburban communities, as well as in certain towns and smaller cities, it is perhaps stronger than it ever was; in larger cities congregations dwindle, and in many country towns no new generation of worshipers is being raised up to fill the pews which the gray-haired will soon vacate.

A recent study of "One Thousand City Churches," published under the auspices of the Institute of Social and Religious Research, shows that "sixty-two per cent. of all ministers reporting have less than $3,000 salary, while five per cent. have less than one thousand dollars." A study of the philanthropic gifts of a typical city (New Haven) conducted by the National Bureau of Economic Research indicates that giving has increased with the country's growth in prosperity, though hardly proportionately, and points out that while gifts to education and various social agencies have shown tremendous gains, the income of religious organizations has experienced a decline since 1923. And this in years when the average American family has more money, beyond its actual needs, than ever before.

Theological seminaries complain of the lack of strong candidates for the ministry. Commissions multiply. Organization increases. Conventions and councils are held, and divide over doctrinal differences. There is tumult and shouting, but no growth in power. And a very large number of the best men and women in the land—a total of several millions probably—who were raised in the church and still retain formal membership, neither attend its services nor participate in its activities. Many are critical; most are merely indifferent. Even the most loyal defenders will hardly claim that it is doing more than holding its own. Pessimists study its statistics and plot its curves and say that it is doomed.

The business in which I am engaged is called upon frequently to survey the markets of manufacturers, discover obstacles, and help in the formation of sound policies on which progress may be based. Can the same sort of thinking contribute anything to the solution of the church's problem? I do not know.

The church, through the ages, has tended to have an unsympathetic attitude toward business. That attitude arose from a misapprehension.

Christianity was launched as a short-time religion. Its first preachers were men who believed that the world was coming very promptly to an end; that it would be liquidated by God as a failure within their own lifetimes. For this belief they had, as they supposed, the highest authority. Starting out among the doomed masses of humanity with this idea, these earliest Christians naturally looked upon any one engaged in business with a feeling of pity, if not contempt. Why tend a store when all stores were so shortly to be closed forever? Why manage a bank when the faithful were presently to be transported to a city whose very streets are paved with gold? Why pretend that the making and exchange of goods is important when all such activities will so quickly cease? The man who stayed with his work under such conditions, neglecting his preparations for eternity, was obviously a fool.

Those first Christians grew old and died like other men, and the hope of a quick millennium flickered but it did not go out. At frequent intervals it burst into flame again, and as the year 1000 drew near all Europe was swept by the conviction that the end was at hand. Men hurried to sell their businesses and turn the proceeds over to the church. Women neglected their children for the more pressing duties of salvation; normal life was almost paralyzed by the eager rush for Heaven.

There are still certain sects of Christians who regard the second coming of Jesus as imminent. Most of us have a different point of view. We see the human race, not old and nearing its end, but new, so new that it has not yet learned to function intelligently. It has hardly conquered famine; it has not even begun to conquer war.

That God should summarily wind it up when it
has solved none of its problems, achieved no
conceivable objective, would be a sad confession
either that He had no definite purpose in beginning it or that the purpose has failed completely.
The millennium is a long way off. Most
Christians now believe that. But the attitude of
the first Christians toward business reflected
itself down through the ages and still influences
the point of view of many sermons.

Business is a necessary function, the sermons
grudgingly admit; the race must be fed and
clothed and housed. But the processes of business are selfish and the only objective money
gain. What men do in their factories and offices
during the week is necessarily compromising.
On Sunday they must go to church to be spiritually cleansed and disinfected in order that they
may go back again into the germ-laden air of
their work.

Was this the attitude of Jesus? Not as I
understand it. He drew no line between service
and religious service. To Him all honest work
was worship, all days Sabbaths, and all houses
temples. He spent far more time in market-
places than in synagogues. He picked His
disciples from the ranks of business. He said to
the woman of Samaria: "It makes no differ-

ence whether you worship God in the temple or in your sacred mountain, or in either place. God is a spirit to be worshiped in the spirit and daily expression of your life." Business, in His eyes, was the machinery which God had set up for carrying on the unfinished task of creation. He denounced greed and broke up the unholy traffic between corrupt business and a corrupt church by hurling the money changers out of the temple, but He made it perfectly clear that a man's first obligation is to provide for his own and for those less fortunate than himself, and that this is a holy work.

The salvation of the modern world depends upon the mutual understanding, and reaction upon each other, of business and the church. Unless business discovers and holds steadily before its eyes a spiritual ideal, unless it thinks more and more in terms of human service, then the net result of its increasing efficiency and profits will be only increasing envy, covetousness and discontent. And the church, unless it learns some of the lessons that business has been forced to learn in the keenly competitive conditions under which it must exist, will not measure up to its new opportunities.

What are some of the lessons which the church could learn from business? With considerable diffidence, because I am well aware of the dangers of the subject, yet with assurance also, for these thoughts were not born yesterday, I present five concrete suggestions.

1. In one important respect the church can learn honesty from business.

Among my friends are members of the Board of Directors of the largest business of its kind in the world. When they came into control of that concern it had on its balance sheet tremendous inventories of raw materials which were carried at cost, though the current market was much lower; it had a number of plants built to manufacture products that had proved unprofitable or unsuitable for the line. It had certain outstanding models which never ought to have been put on the market but yet represented an investment of millions. In the first year of its new management that great company wrote off from its books more than thirty-eight million dollars. The result was very small earnings for that year and no dividends for the stockholders. I asked one of the directors why it had been decided to absorb the whole loss in a single year; wouldn't it have been wiser perhaps to spread the write-off over a longer period?

His answer was an emphatic, "No. We were determined to cut to the bone," he said.

"We wanted to get all the bad news as fast as we could and clear away everything about which there could be any possible doubt. Then we knew that what was left was solid, and on that we could begin to build."

That is the habit of sound business. It is not the habit of the church. The statistics which are issued by the churches are not sincere statistics; they do not give an accurate picture. There is hardly a church membership roll anywhere that does not carry as active members a large percentage of people who are no longer active. Some have ceased to attend; some have moved away; some have been lost from sight entirely. Yet their names continue to be carried and go to swell the misleading totals which give the annual impression that the church is gaining, or at least holding its own, when one has only to drop into a Sunday morning service to learn the contrary.

I have said that in my own business we are called upon frequently to study the sales problems of a manufacturer. We conduct what we call market surveys, and our first objective in such a survey is to uncover grief. We ask *first:* "What is the matter with this product? Why do not more people buy it? Where are the people who used to buy it and no longer do? What

189

Is their complaint? Why did they switch to something else? What can the manufacturer do, if anything, to win them back? Is the product perhaps unsuitable to the present market? Have conditions changed since it was first marketed, and has it failed to keep pace with the change? Should it be altered? Should it perhaps be withdrawn altogether and something different substituted in its place?"

The manufacturer knows without any help from us the strong points of his position. He asks us to find his troubles and propose a remedy. And when, after such a study, we come back to him with criticisms, complaints, signs of failure on the part of his organization, indications that he has been too complacent while his competition has been more aggressive, we present the report with no sense of embarrassment. It may not make good reading, but there is no suspicion in the mind of the manufacturer that we are unfriendly. No cry is raised that we are impious, that we are attacking the sacred citadels of business.

Has there ever been on the part of the church a thoroughgoing effort at a similar survey? The church itself could hardly make it, for people hesitate to hurt feelings; they like to tell a pastor what he likes to hear. But an organization trained in survey work could, and the results would be illuminating even though they were confined to only half a dozen communities. "What does every man in this town think of the church? Why is he not availing himself of its service? Why does he feel no call to contribute to it? In what way could the service of the church be modified so that it would appeal to him?" Such a study would bring out much that would be unpleasant reading. It would result in a considerable elimination of names from the membership roll; it would "cut to the bone." But when it was finished the church, too, would know its problems and on what exactly it had to build.

The famous Doctor Jameson, when he was about to set forth on his hazardous and, as it proved, unsuccessful raid, received a telegram from Cecil Rhodes. It said simply: "Read Luke 14:31."

Calling for a Bible, Doctor Jameson turned to the passage and found these words: "Or what king, going to make war against another king, sitteth not down first, and consulteth whether he be able with ten thousand to meet him that cometh against him with twenty thousand?"

A businesslike injunction, that verse, a sturdy insistence on facing the hard facts, on getting all the bad news first. The words were spoken by Jesus.

2. It sounds almost shocking, yet it is true, that in some respects the church does not have as much faith as business.

Few institutions are more impressive than the research laboratories of a great industrial organization. You pass through the door of such a laboratory into another world. Here are scientists, not business men. There is no talk of money, no chatter of the ticker, no gossip of trades and profit or loss. No hurry and no fear. You have the feeling that these men are concerned with forces and events beyond the horizon of every-day life. They are the mystics of the modern world. They have no master but the truth.

I have in mind one such laboratory whose annual budget is upward of two million dollars a year. The two millions are provided by a very practical business organization, which exists to sell goods at a profit and pay dividends to its stockholders. The officers of that corporation know that at any hour of the day those scientists may appear at headquarters with some such announcement as this: "We have discovered a new and better process. It will mean the junking of twenty million dollars' worth of your present

machinery." Or, "We have found a better way
to do the things that you have been doing. It
will mean closing two of your factories and con-
solidating a half-dozen departments, but it will
put you in shape to render better service." Or,
"We are compelled to tell you that you will have
to plan to withdraw one of your principal products from the market. We have discovered
something much finer to take its place."

Some such bomb shell as this may be ex-
ploded in the executive offices by the scientists at
any hour. Do the executives try to shield themselves from that possibility? On the contrary,
they spend two millions a year in order to
provoke it. They are absolutely sure of one
thing and one thing only, and that is *change*.
They can not tell you what to-morrow's business
problems and developments will be but they can
prophesy definitely that they will be different
from those of yesterday and to-day. They have
only one fear—that the future may spring upon
them suddenly and find them unprepared.

Business *knows* that to-morrow is going to be
different; the church is too often merely *afraid*
that it may be. There is the gulf between them.
The church trembles at anything that looks like
change. It sticks to the old methods, believing
them sacred because they are old. It wears out

the energies of the pastor in maintaining a mid-week prayer service to which none but a few of the super-righteous come. It must have a Sunday evening service because it always has had such a service, and to give it up would look as if the church were losing ground. It "must maintain its work," and in the puff and flurry of that effort it too often does not stop to ask: "Is this work, which was a service when it was instituted a hundred years ago, a service now? Or could our energy be turned to other and more useful channels?"

A hundred years from now there may be no railroads. It is unlikely but not inconceivable. Goods and passengers may very possibly be carried through the air, where the right of way is free and requires no upkeep. Are the railroads disturbed by such a suggestion? Go into their research departments and you will doubtless find them right now busy with experiments to determine just what air transport can be made to do.

A hundred years from now there may be no newspapers. Again, conceivable but hardly probable. All news may possibly be flashed by radio directly on to the walls of the individual home. Are the newspapers panicky at such an outlook? If and when the change comes the better papers will have seen it so far ahead that they will be able to make the shift almost over night. They are not wedded to printing presses and ink, the altars and sacraments of their present era. Take these away and they will build new altars out of the lightning and the ether waves.

Business knows that under any kind of conditions there will be business to be done. For there will be people, and they will have wants. And business is merely the function of satisfying wants.

A hundred years from now there may be no church service in the sense of a meeting together of people for worship. Should that possibility disturb the church? Surely not. Surely it can afford to be as brave as business. For a hundred years from now there will still be God and there will still be people, and the church, if it be anything, is the linking of people with God.

3. Stated in another way, business is endlessly flexible and adaptable; the church is too often rigid and unadaptable. I speak now particularly of the Protestant Church; the Roman Catholic Church has shown a deeper knowledge of human nature and more capacity for giving the people what the people really need.

WHAT CAN A MAN BELIEVE?

Let us take the typical Sunday morning service as an example. When and how did it originate? It originated in times when people lived on farms, far from one another, and were engaged in work that kept them isolated through the week. It was outdoor work and healthy, but it was lonesome and physically tiring. It gave little chance for social companionship or intellectual development; people were hungry for both, so hungry that they drove into church on Sunday morning and stayed in and around the church all day. They were starving; they could not get enough. And the pastor, who was the one man of leisure in the community, the one man who bought books and subscribed to periodicals, often the only man who received a newspaper, was their news-giver, their librarian, their theater, their moving picture, their whole intellectual bill of fare.

In a century conditions have undergone a complete change. Isolation has been banished by the growth of cities, the development of railroads, and the coming of the automobile. We no longer work through the week far apart and in the open air. We are crowded together in offices and factories; jostled continuously against other people; forced into the closest kind of contact with everybody *except* the members of our own families—our children and our wives. Our hunger on Sunday is not for gregariousness but for separation, for a little time to be away from the world, to be with our own people, alone.

It is for this reason, and not because religion is dying out in the world, that the Sunday morning service is maintained with so much effort. The church is not the only sufferer by the change. Political parties have not been able to hold really successful rallies in this country for many years. The membership lists of even the most "exclusive" clubs are often less than full, and the club houses ordinarily deserted except for those few homeless bachelors and grass-widowers who have nowhere else to go. Meetings are on the toboggan. We are fed up with people during the week; on Sunday we hunger for freedom. We are stifled indoors throughout the week; on Sundays we hunger for the open air. And such intellectual hunger as we have has a thousand feeding places. We buy all the new books as fast as the pastor does. The new magazines reach us and him on the same day. Unless he be an unusual man there is not much news he can give to our minds. We are abreast of him mentally; often ahead.

Thus the church becomes reduced to its primary function. It is no longer necessary as a

social center; it is no longer an intellectual headquarters. It can be and should be still a
headquarters for spiritual inspiration, an oasis
of reverence, a giver of peace. The Catholic
Church fulfills this primary function. It does
not demand that its people shall sit down together for very long. It does not preempt the
very middle of Sunday and set itself rigidly
there, spoiling both the morning and the afternoon for those who seek the open air. It acts
on the principle that the church is made for the
people and not people for the church. From
early in the morning until late at night it keeps
its doors open and repeats its masses. And early
or late one may step through the door and bow
his head and come forth with the assurance that
he has been put into touch with God. The rest of
the day is his own, to be used in rest or in
pleasure, as should be gratifying to a Father who
smiles when His children are glad.

The Catholic Church makes little of the sermon; to it the Protestant Church subordinates
everything else. I am writing this particular
paragraph on Sunday afternoon after having attended morning service. The pastor of the
church was absent, preaching at a college, and
the assistant pastor, a rosy-cheeked boy,
preached for three-quarters of an hour on the

disappointments of Jesus. A nice little boy who has never in his life had any disappointments. He had poetry quotations in his sermons and references to great books and famous lives, but hardly a line that connected it up with our present-day living. Nothing to give the slightest suggestion that he himself had ever felt anything, hoped anything, feared anything. One wondered what an assistant pastor does or thinks through the week. For all the reflection of daily life in his talk he might have been just a rosy-cheeked visitor from Mars.

On other Sundays I have stopped in at the Russian Cathedral which is not far from my house and stood with bared head listening to the deep bass notes of its glorious chants. There is no sermon; I do not understand a single word. Yet somehow the thing in me which is mystic feels satisfied. I have the sense that this old old ritual reaches back to the very beginnings of faith and stretches forward and upward beyond the present. That somehow there is understanding and healing in that service which for hundreds of years has wrapped itself protectingly around the souls of men. I am a Protestant of a score of generations. It is impossible for me intellectually to be a Catholic; spiritually I wish often that I could be.

4. Business checks up on itself frequently to be sure that it still is headed for its original goals. Is there not need for a similar check-up on the part of the church? Has it not somehow managed, in the corrosion of the ages, to get itself turned around so that the emphasis of Jesus is reversed?

What is the outstanding fact about His attitude toward people? He genuinely liked them. He was happy when they were happy. He feasted and dined, and when He called a new disciple that one made a celebration of it which was so miscellaneous and noisy that it shocked the pious. He insisted that little children be allowed to come to Him when the more self-important of His disciples would have kept them away. He stopped to heal a blind man when he was on His way to Jerusalem to be crucified. He liked people to be happy. And He treated them very tenderly, like erring children, when they made mistakes.

The disciples broke the Sabbath laws and indulged in too much walking, the only kind of Sabbath athletics that existed in those days. Did He denounce them? He was with them. The guests at a country wedding were warm and joyous from their wine. Did He rise frowning in the midst to rebuke their merriment? He contributed to it. The woman taken in adultery had merited stoning under the church law. Did He say: "It is a harsh law, but I must support the established institutions. There can be no half-way measures in dealing with this sin"? He shamed her accusers out of the room and, lifting her tenderly to her feet, bade her go and sin no more.

To the natural, normal, human frailties of men and women, the frailties that arise out of the eager, child-like desire to catch a fleeting moment of happiness in this rather cruel world, Jesus of Nazareth showed an amazing pity and forgiveness. But He denounced with words as bitter as any that have ever been spoken the sins that make life harder for other people, the respectable, profitable sins—greed and selfishness and oppression. For these He had no forgiveness. Harlots and publicans shall enter into the Kingdom of Heaven, but Pharisees, unjust lawyers, grinders of the poor, rich men who have coined their fortunes out of human sweat and blood—these have no place in the presence of God. They have robbed life of its joy for His children.

Too often the church has got it all turned around. Rich men, greedy men, hard-hearted men are in its ranks and often in positions of authority and honor. And the great forces of its organized power are exerted for what? To keep people who like wine and who consider that there is no moral wrong in drinking it from having any. To suppress Sunday games. To be very bitter and unforgiving toward the girl who yields to the impulses of hot blood. These things, which Jesus regarded as of less importance, have become the law and the prophets. And the other and greater sins go usually unrebuked.

It is not the purpose of this book to quarrel with creeds. In some ways they serve a very useful purpose. But we venture to raise the point that most creeds are more interested in speculating about the nature of Jesus than they are in finding out what Jesus Himself believed. And where Christians quarrel, their quarrels are usually about matters in which He displayed no interest.

To the very righteous of His own day He was not a religious man. It is interesting to wonder if He would be so regarded to-day. He knew, to be sure, that there had to be some sort of church organization, for He remarked that the gates of Hell should not prevail against His church; but I do not discover that He showed any interest in organization details. He paid a certain amount of attention to His duties as a member of the Jewish Church and was jealous for the purity of the Temple, but He did not observe the Passover in the form that Moses prescribed; Moses had said that the Passover must be eaten standing, in haste, and with sandals on the feet. He ate it reclining, with bare feet, and at great leisure. He was not deliberately defying the law; He simply did not care about those details.

What did He really care for?

As stated again and again in this book, He cared for people. When the rich young ruler came to Him, asking what he should do to be saved, Jesus recited the commandments that have to do with human relations, omitting all those that prescribe men's duties to God. I imagine that very few modern Christians would have done this, and that if any one other than Jesus had done it, the list of commandments would have been considered fatally defective. He did not think He was leaving God out when He put humanity first.

Jesus treated human life as normal and important. He cared for men in their labor, for women in their backaches, for little children in their sorrows and joys. He believed that a wedding was a proper place for Him to be and remain. He was willing if necessary to be criticized for the extent to which He enjoyed festivity. He treated all human life as if it had a value and as if religion was expressed in it. He cared whether men got paid for their work or not. A large proportion of His parables had to do with commercial transactions. One of the most generally accepted of the non-canonical sayings of Jesus, believed in by many of the early church fathers, was: "Prove yourselves tried money changers," reliable men, and judges of sound values.

He cared for mercy, not sacrifice; justice, not ritual.

And He wanted men to believe that God was to be found in the shop as well as in the temple. Indeed, it may be questioned if there be a truer verse in the Book of Revelation than that in which John, viewing the Holy City, looks around in vain for a temple, because there *all* life is religious.

Is His attitude the church's attitude? Is its emphasis placed where He placed His? These are the questions which are vital—more vital than any creeds.

5. Any business is terrifically concerned if there be the slightest depreciation in the quality of the men who enter its ranks. The leading

corporations of the country send emissaries every year to the colleges to spy out the leaders and to seek to apprentice them. Money is nothing; it is so cheap that any man with an idea and courage can get all he wants of it. Buildings are as likely to be a liability as an asset. Patents, processes, distribution—all easy. But men, men, men! There can be no permanent business success with poor men.

Church leaders have frequently deplored the fact that the ministry no longer attracts the strongest men. A hundred years ago the best men in every college headed for the pulpit; it was the place of power. Fifty years ago some of the best men and many of the good men became preachers. For the past twenty years the record has been a declining one, both in quantity and quality. Hundreds of churches have no pastors at all, while the few outstanding men in the pulpit are constantly engaged in declining invitations to move. Of the men who were in college when I was only one leader went into the ministry. Naturally he moved straight to the top, and big city churches have been bidding for him with one another since his thirtieth year.

The church must have better leaders; all its friends are in agreement on that. Why doesn't it get them? For many reasons, probably, that are beyond our present analysis, but for two reasons of which we can speak with definite conviction.

First, because of the archaic and absurd hurdles that are put up to keep strong men from the ministry—the traditional emphasis upon creed. A convention of ministers gathers to examine candidates, and what is the first question? Frequently it is: "Do you believe in the Virgin Birth?" This is an important part of church doctrine for many people, but was it important to Jesus? The record does not say so. Did He stand at the door of Matthew's feast and stop all comers, saying: "Just a minute. Do you believe in the Virgin Birth? If not, you may not enter." Did he say: "Come unto me all ye that are weary and believe in the Virgin Birth and I will give you rest?"

When he called Philip, that eager disciple went out immediately and hunted up his brother Nathaniel and said: "We have found him of whom Moses in the law and the prophets did write, Jesus of Nazareth, the son of Joseph." Did Jesus rebuke Philip? He did not. If the Virgin Birth were important to His mind, the disciples never mentioned it. Two of the writers of the Gospels do not refer to it; Paul, the great apostle, apparently never heard of it. Yet it occupies whole days in church conventions, dividing men into bitter factions and keeping young men out of the ranks of the ministry.

What sort of questions would Jesus be likely to ask of candidates if He were examining them in such a church convocation? Speaking very reverently, it seems as if He might be interested in points like these:

"Could you conduct a successful carpenter shop or fishing business? Have you demonstrated that you can make a success of any business?"

He chose His first disciples from the ranks of business. They had demonstrated that they could order their lives successfully. Also they understood the lives and problems, the hopes and fears and difficulties of common folks because they themselves had shared the common lot.

"You are going into the business of life at the top," He might say. "You are essaying the highest and most difficult of all human endeavor. Would it not be wise for you first to demonstrate your capacity to handle little things before reaching up for the greatest?

"Do little children love you and follow you around?

"Do sick people feel better or worse when you come into the room?

207

WHAT CAN A MAN BELIEVE?

"Have you any conviction about the importance of your message which would make you believe that five thousand people would go out into the country to hear you preach, forgetting to take their lunch?"

These are sensible questions. They reach down toward the sources of Jesus' own power and success. He would be a strong, self-reliant man indeed who would answer them all in the affirmative. But the church is presumed to be seeking self-reliant men. Its present creedal tests are not always calculated to select them.

And the present conditions of its service do not attract them. That is the second fact which seems self-evident.

To be the private chaplain of twenty-five or fifty families; to make pastoral calls and attend meetings of women's auxiliaries; to conduct a prayer meeting for a dozen completely saved and sanctified old people; to live shabbily and be worried about the education of the children and the burdens of old age—this is not the life to appeal to a high spirited man. There is no lift in it, no power, nothing to tempt a man to trade for it the only life on earth that he will ever have.

All over the country are thousands of faithful country parsons whose lives are being worn out under the conditions set forth. They are not to

blame. The church called them to great things
and it has given them only very little things.
Many of them are baffled and almost hopeless,
caught in the toils of a situation from which
there seems no escape. They feel they are living
at only half capacity, yet are powerless to do
more. One sympathizes with them, but one is
compelled to recognize frankly that so long as
their situation is what it is strong young men are
not going to flock into the ministry.

On the positive side, it should be emphasized
that the church has a greater recuperative
power, a more vigorous resiliency than any other
institution in the world. Indeed, the best proof
of its divine origin is not creed or tradition, but
its amazing capacity for withstanding the blows
dealt to it by its friends.

Read the epistles of St. Paul and the other
apostles; what do they contain? Much doctrinal
guidance, much inspiration, much spiritual food.
But with all this, much reproach and exhortation.
Paul has heard with dismay that there is a church
squabble in this city, that another congregation
is growing lax, that a third is being seduced by
the pleasures of the pagan world. Take those
passages out of the letters and put them all
together, and they make a picture of religious

conditions almost as sad as any that a modern alarmist could paint.

The Middle Ages, outwardly so dominated by the church, were spiritually barren, soiled by greed and disgraced by ignorance and intolerance. Even in the times of our great-grandparents, which we are accustomed to regard as the "good old days," the tide of religious interest ebbed and flowed. In the year 1800, there was only one professing Christian in the student body of Yale. So religion has always been on trial; the church always fighting a hard battle, "truth forever on the scaffold, wrong forever on the throne."

That great thinker and prophet, Professor Rauschenbusch, once stood before a cosmopolitan audience to deliver an address on the social aspects of Christianity. He was interrupted at the very outset by a Socialist who climbed on to a chair and launched a bitter attack against the church. Professor Rauschenbusch, who was very deaf, waited patiently and, when the chairman had given him the import of the disturber's remarks, spoke only a single sentence of comment.

"Nobody kicks a dead horse," he said quietly, and proceeded to deliver his paper.

He was right. Nobody does kick a dead horse; nobody takes the trouble to attack a man or an institution from which life has departed. So long as vigorous and even emphatic discussion goes on inside the church and outside, you may be sure that the church is still very much alive.

Moreover, discussion and even disagreement are inherent in the very nature of Christianity. The early church had hardly begun its existence when a serious doctrinal controversy broke out. Paul, who was not one of the original twelve, had been in far countries teaching the Gentiles, and criticisms about him drifted back to Jerusalem. He was allowing converts to join the church without insisting on certain rites which the stricter disciples held essential. A conference was called. Paul made his defense, and a tolerant working arrangement was arrived at. In Jerusalem they would continue to teach the strict doctrine, but out in the missionary fields Paul was to be allowed such latitude as the different conditions seemed to require. So the two factions agreed to disagree with mutual affection and respect.

The Jerusalem church was presided over by James, the brother of Jesus, who seems not to have believed on Him during His lifetime but to have been somehow won over after His death and elevated, because of his relationship, to this place of authority. He lived a noble life and died, traditionally, a martyr's death, but it is interesting to note that his part of the church, which was in Jerusalem and held rigidly to the form of the law, refusing to change or adapt, ceased to grow and soon died out. It was the churches established by Paul, the first heretic, which lived and spread and conquered the world. That fact has both significance and encouragement in the present situation. Significance because it shows that without change comes death. Encouragement as proving the vitality of a gospel which can take root in hostile soil and grow and spread until it overshadows even the empire itself.

In a previous chapter we dealt impersonally with the history of the church, setting forth its failures and seeking to strike a balance between its sins and its services. We concluded that it deserves to survive, that, granting its critics the strongest possible case, it still remains the inspiration of democracy, benevolence and high ideals. In this chapter, which has dealt very frankly with the shortcomings of the current situation, as a business man's survey would reveal them, we desire to conclude by reaffirming that conviction. The church can not and will not die. Men are, as they always have been, "incurably religious." There is in each human being what Oliver Wendell Holmes discovered in himself, a little plant called reverence that demands watering at least once a week. The church has the waters of eternal life. The obligation of those who seek a better world is not to stand outside and criticize but to stay inside and work for more courageous thinking, a greater willingness to discard the useless, and a larger faith. A faith which believes in God enough to be very sure that even if most of the forms and ceremonies which we think of as traditional church "service" should pass out of the picture a nobler and more serviceable church will inevitably arise.

In what form might that nobler church appear? If we could look a hundred years into the future, what sort of church should we see? These are questions beyond any human power to answer. He who essays the rôle of prophet finds himself generally discredited and ridiculous. Yet we have not hesitated to say positively that the church of the future will be very different from the church of to-day, and there is a certain obligation on us, perhaps, to indicate in broad outline what, in our imagination, might come to pass.

Let us, then, for a moment cast aside all fear

and allow our imagination to run riot. It is only by this process that the scientists make their great discoveries and improvements.

I know one of these scientists. He is associated with a great industry. They gave him one day the problem of reducing the cost of automobiles by shortening the time necessary to put an automobile body through the paint shops. It required at that period thirty-five days to put the finish on a fine body, for each coat of varnish had to dry and be baked before the next coat could be applied.

He said: "What we ought to look for is a finish that can be applied in an hour."

They laughed him to scorn, but he stuck to his point.

"If you start out to make a ten per cent. improvement in any situation you will make no improvement," he insisted. "But if you start out to make a hundred per cent. improvement, or a five hundred per cent. improvement, you may achieve the ten per cent."

The result of that sort of thinking, plus an endless amount of patient research, was a new automobile finish which dries so quickly that it can not be spread on with a brush, as in the old days, but must be squirted under pressure from a hose. The problem was solved; the neck of the bottle of automobile production, which was the paint shop, was opened, and all car owners are driving better automobiles at lower prices because of the immense reduction in costs which was thus achieved.

Let us try for a moment to apply that sort of audacious thinking to the possible future of the church.

There is a town, let us say, of five thousand people. It has one Catholic Church, with which we are not concerned, for it is doing the task which it was set up to do; it is holding its members and keeping their children. There are six Protestant Churches, and none of them is doing well. The pews, which once were full on Sunday, are now only one-third full, or worse. The physical condition of the buildings is not good; they need redecorating inside and out. Budgets are raised with considerable difficulty. A group of older people continue faithful, and the Sunday-schools render real service, but the generation of folk between twenty and forty-five rides in automobiles on Sunday, or plays golf or fusses around the house or reads.

Judged either as intellectual food or spiritual stimulus, the sermons average low. It is not strange. No man can be inspired who faces half-empty pews. In tone the preaching is earnest, but there is an unhappy undercurrent, as though the preachers themselves wonder whether it is quite worth while. Many sermons are offered on "What is the matter with the church?" and kindred subjects. Every year one or another of the churches seeks by lectures or motion pictures or a brass band to put life into the evening service. These efforts are not a sustained success. Among the pastors there is considerable talk of a religious revival, a new statement of religion, a fresh interpretation that will reach out and grip the modern man and woman. The revival is delayed. Meanwhile, the program of the churches is about what it always has been, a morning service at eleven o'clock, an evening service at seven, a prayer meeting on Wednesday evening, a Sunday-school and a young people's society. The measure of strength and influence is: How many people can we induce to attend?

The pastors are tragically underpaid. Their salaries were as good as any in town a century ago, but they have not been raised, and the cost of living has soared.

Things may get better in this imaginary town of ours. The belated revival may arrive. A great awakening of some sort may send the people flocking back to the pews and restore the pulpits to their old place of leadership, all without any radical change of program. This is one possibility and needs no elaboration. Let us face courageously the other possibility. Suppose things do not get better, but rather worse. What might happen in such a town?

Well, this might happen. The pastors might gather in a secret and confidential meeting. They might say to one another: "The time has come for us to sit down frankly and face the facts. To our congregations, of course, we have had to show a bold front; we have had to hope that the great new day is just around the corner. But if we are to make any progress we must not have any pretense among ourselves. What is the situation?

"The town is more prosperous than it ever was. Its people are busy and, on the whole, happy. The standards of business are infinitely higher than they were when the church was in the saddle. No present-day business man would ever think of investing money in the slave trade or the rum trade. Yet deacons of the church were once eminent in both. Children are better fed and better cared for in every way. Health is better. Schools are better. More money is spent on the relief of sickness and old age. Life is more comfortable, more healthful and more

217

worth while for the great body of the inhabitants than it ever has been. All this looks as if God is making progress with His plans. For surely the end of His plan is a happy, kindly, sympathetic and hopeful race. *He* progresses, but *the church* does not. Why this seeming contradiction? Let us go into the town and find out.

"Let us put it up frankly to the business men. Let us say to them: 'You believe in God. You want your children to grow up believing. Not a man of you would want to live or do business in a town without a church. You must, therefore, want some sort of church, but it appears that you do not want the kind which we are conducting for you. At least you do not want it enough to support it. All right, what kind of church would serve this community? It is your town, not ours. Suppose you disregard all tradition, forget everything that now exists, including even us preachers, and tell us what kind of church would render a service of which people would feel sufficient need so that they would support it.' "

We shall suppose that something like this takes place in our imaginary town, and that the situation begins to go through a process of evolution. Experiments are tried and improvements made. Years pass. A hundred years. Let us look at the town again.

It is a very much better-looking town. A hundred years of industrial progress have produced a great deal of wealth which, while it is still unevenly divided, is sufficiently spread around so that everybody has a comfortable home, good clothes and the ability to provide education for the children. Machinery has been so perfected, and electrical power utilized to such an extent, that the work, both in the factories and in the homes, is done in five or six hours, and there is leisure for everybody. Indeed, the so-called economic struggle is over. Money is, as the bankers say, "cheap." It is so cheap that it is no longer a ruling consideration in men's minds. Since everybody has enough, nobody is particularly worried about getting more. The profit motive is still important, but pride in service rendered has become even more important. Men are very jealous of the reputation of their businesses and have toward their daily occupations a feeling of real reverence. To be merely wealthy is no longer a distinction, since every one is comparatively wealthy. But excellence in service is eagerly sought and rewarded with honor.

Medical science has almost banished pain. You are impressed, as you walk the streets, with the happiness in the faces of the people. They enjoy their lives. They keep young a long time and when they die there are tears in the eyes of those left behind but no despair in their hearts. The cemetery on the edge of the town has been radically transformed. All of the monuments have been removed. It is no longer the ghastly stone yard of the past but a beautiful park, where the graves are marked by simple tablets laid flat in the grass. Doves fly over it, and children play in it. Every detail and symbol speaks not of death but of life. The inhabitants of that town think of their loved ones as living, not dead; and a funeral service consists usually of a dinner where the pastor and one or two intimate friends speak appreciatively of the friend who has gone. Good stories are often told at these dinners. Believing in immortality, these people, curiously enough, act as if they believed.

Instead of the six churches that struggled for existence, there is one church. In the rear of it is a Sunday-school building which is used for the religious instruction of the youth, and for nothing else. No entertainments are held in it, no bazaars, no motion-picture shows. The church attempts to do nothing which other agencies can do as well or better. It confines itself exclusively to the one thing which no other institution can do, the spiritual training and inspiration of the people.

The church building itself is not large, for very few people attend any single service. It is open all day, and men and women drop in at various times, sit down for a few minutes, listen to the great organ which is played all day long, kneel in silent prayer, and go out. Religion is accepted as a perfectly normal part of life; or, to state it more accurately, is regarded *as* life. Men pray as they breathe or eat or take their morning exercise. That there is a spiritual side to their natures, they know, and they know it must be fed.

Every home, office, factory and store has its radio, of course, and its device for receiving by radio the pictures of any distant person or scene and projecting them on the wall. So on entering an office a few minutes before nine o'clock you are met by an interesting and impressive ceremony. A strain of music greets your ears, the voice of a great church organ. It is followed by a moment of silence, and then there appears on the wall the figure of the pastor standing in his pulpit. He makes a very simple little prayer, the kind of a prayer which Nehemiah (who wasn't a prophet but just a business man) used to make on beginning his day's work at the rebuilding of Jerusalem. Nehemiah was busy, and so conscious that his work was God's work that he felt it unnecessary to keep running to Heaven with either pleas or praise. He simply bowed his head and said, "Prosper, I pray thee, thy servant this day," and forthwith started operations. So the prayer of the pastor in our town is a simple prayer, but the whole town pauses for it, and the day's work starts with the reminder that work is service, honest, useful, cheerful service—religious service.

The pastor himself is a remarkable character. He wears no special uniform, but you would not need to have him pointed out in order to know that he is a pastor. His face reveals it; there is something in his expression which proclaims him as a confident citizen of two worlds. He is about fifty years of age, for no man reaches the ministry in these days until he is well on toward forty. It is recognized as the greatest and most honored of all the professions, and one must have proved superior qualities in business or professional work before even being admitted into training. The training consists of a study of the Bible and particularly the life of Christ, followed by two or three years of travel, part of it in the Orient, where mysticism has always had its home, and men find it somehow easier to forget themselves in the contemplation of the Infinite.

A pastor comes from that training with the glow of the other world about him. He comes not to *do* something, or to *say* something, but to *be* something. Men feel his presence the minute they enter the room. There is strength in the very touch of him, as there was healing in the hem of the garment of the Lord. As he is not required to preach often or speak at every sort of public function, he is not driven back into the dusty companionship of books; he seems always to have plenty of time. So children flock around him whenever he appears, and every home and office feels hallowed by his presence.

He has power to perform miracles, to feed the hungry and cure the sick, power through money. A generous fund is given into his hands every year, and when there is a sick man who needs medical attention, or a child whose teeth should be straightened, or a family that has had bad luck, the pastor provides. He renders no accounting, and the distribution of the help is made so quietly that none except the doctors know where or how it has been done. Needless to say, his own family's needs are amply provided for; his children are educated and started in life, and all worry of old age removed from the minds of his wife and himself. They have no private cares of their own at all, but the community casts its spiritual burdens upon their shoulders, and they bear them gladly.

On Sunday the pastor conducts three short services in the morning, beginning at six o'clock, and three in the late afternoon and evening. One may go at any time, and having bowed his head and knelt and listened to the organ and the prayers, may pass out into the sunshine and rejoice in the day. On rare occasions, such as Christmas and Easter, he preaches, and his sermons are masterpieces—the fruit of his whole experience of living and reading and thought. As such they are eagerly sought by the community. But his primary function is to be pastor and priest. People come to him in the sanctity of his study with their troubles, their worries, and their sins; and when he says to them: "Your Father has forgiven you, go and sin no more," they know that he *knows*. At the time of the noonday meal and at supper time, he stands at his altar and, through the magic of the radio and of "television," he stands also in every home and lifts to Heaven the community's thanks. Throughout the town there is happiness and cheer and hope because he passes by.

Once a year there is a town meeting, and he makes a report. A curious sort of church report it is. It says nothing of attendance at meet-

ings, of amounts collected, of numbers added to
the church. For the town is the church and the
church is the town, and all, being children of the
Father, are born into the fold. No, the report
speaks of quite other matters: of the improvements in the community health and the lowered
infant mortality. Of the betterments in the
schools; of the steady employment in the offices
and factories; of the gifts that the town has made
to less fortunate people in other places and
lands; of the good record that the town's boys
and girls are making in the cities; of the moral
courage of some who have undergone difficulties
with cheerfulness; of the fine hope with which
others have passed beyond the pale. Of everything which indicates that life is better, happier,
more courageous, more Godlike in the
community; everything which indicates that He
who came that men might have life more abundantly is realizing the object for which He came.
This is the sort of report the pastor makes. And
when he has finished, he blesses them all, and
there is a moment's silence. Then the buzz of
happy voices, and the music of children's
laughter.

. . . . .

Is this an impossible picture? I do not think
so. Certainly no one can say that it is "un-

scriptural." Jesus asked: "When the Son of man cometh shall he find faith on the earth?" He did not ask: "Shall He find a morning service at eleven o'clock, an evening service at seven, a mid-week prayer meeting and a young people's society?" But "shall He find faith?" He shall!

CHAPTER VI

THE MAGIC THAT MOVES MOUNTAINS

Some upper classmen assembled one night in a college hall to listen to two speakers. A bishop of distinguished service and great spiritual power was one of them, and a public lecturer, widely advertised as a professional agnostic, was the other. The plan was for each man to present his own philosophy of life. The audience, while not large, was very earnest, and obviously looked for a spirited debate. The bishop spoke first.

Gray-haired now, and a trifle bent, the old man had started his service in the foreign missionary field, and more than once in his youth had risked his life for the faith. On his return to this country he had held influential pastorates in many cities, becoming the friend and confidant of men of every sort. He knew all that there is to know of human hopes and fears, sufferings and joys, achievements and tragedies. Yet his fine face was ruddy and untroubled as the face of a little child. No one who looked at him could doubt that he had, in truth, "cast his burdens upon the Lord."

His tone was deep and sympathetic.

"Nothing that is worth while in life can be proved," he said. "Men speak of depending on science, but science itself depends upon faith. It assumes that 'every effect must have an adequate cause'—a tremendous assumption which no one can prove. It assumes that the world which each man builds up inside his mind corresponds to the outside world of reality, that the universe which you see is the same universe which I see— another great act of faith. All scientific discoveries have been made by men who believed more than their eyes could see or their fingers handle. 'He who does not look beyond the fact,' said Darwin, 'will hardly see the fact,' by which he meant that the eyes of the imagination—of faith—must first see what *may* be before the eyes of the flesh can see what *is*.

"I can not prove to you that there is any purpose behind the universe. It may be that the whole thing is a mere happening, a jest of circumstances; that we and all who have been before us or are to come after us are no more significant than the flies that live their whole existence in a single hour, or the bubbles that appear on the surface of the stream and break and reappear. I can not prove to you that this is not so. But, my friends, no man can prove to you that it *is* so. The existence of Reason behind the universe, or its non-existence, are both beyond the power of finite minds to establish. Since, therefore, the choice is free between the two alternatives, I choose to accept the positive faith. For that faith gives significance to my life and to the lives of all men. It clothes me with conviction. It invests me with the right to go forward with firm step and head erect, as one who shall not perish. In place of worry and fear, it sets up hope and courage. It is the pathway to power."

When he had finished the other speaker rose very slowly and looked down into the eager faces of those young men. He stood silent for what seemed a very long time, searching their eyes.

"I am going to surprise you, my young friends," he said at last. "Perhaps in a sense I shall disappoint you. I am an agnostic. Some of you have come here in the expectation that the Bishop and I should vigorously disagree. You had expected that I should call the great skeptics of history to my aid, and marshal the arguments which seem to prove that man is a creature of the moment, bound for oblivion in death. I confess that this was my purpose when I came.

"But I have changed that purpose. I am going to say only one thing to you young gentlemen. It is this: If you can believe the things that our friend the Bishop has been saying, then, in God's name, believe them! The texture of my mind is such that I myself can not go farther than to say I do not know. If you can go farther, if you can have a positive faith, then with all my heart I congratulate you. I would give anything in the world if I could. For what the Bishop has claimed for his faith is true. Skepticism has no vitality; the motive power of progress is faith."

He sat down, and after a few minutes of rather embarrassed silence the meeting disbanded. The students were surprised, but the Bishop much more so. He had expected a contest. Instead of which he had listened to a testimony far more moving than his own, the almost tragic confession of one whose honest intellect would not let him go a step beyond the things which can be seen and heard and felt, but who looked with hungry yearning into the richer lives of those who can believe and do.

There are probably more honest-minded men in the world to-day than ever before in history. More men whose "word is as good as their bond," who hate hypocrisy, who take a personal delight in being square when nobody is watching. The very thought that they might profit, either in this world or in a possible other world, through professing to believe more than they really do believe, revolts them. They will play out the hand that Fate has dealt, asking no favors. If there shall prove to be something beyond the grave they will stand firmly on their records; if there be nothing, they face that possibility without fear.

For such men principally this book has been written. It has attempted honestly to present both sides. It has established the intelligent man's *right* to believe. In a situation where the evidence on both sides is equal, no one need feel that he violates his intellectual integrity if he chooses the positive rather than the negative side. To this point the preceding chapters have brought us. One last thought remains to be added. It is this: Not only has an intelligent man a right to believe, he is cheating himself if he does not exercise that right.

Cheating himself in many ways, the first of which, perhaps the least important, is in his own business.

As a matter of fact, no man can stay in business except through some measure of faith. It is impossible even to discuss business without using that word again and again. You hear men say: "The whole modern commercial structure is built on a foundation of credit." And what is the word credit; where does it come from? *Credo: I believe.* Business is good or bad, the statisticians point out, according to the degree of confidence. What is confidence? Whence comes the word? *Con-fides: with faith.* "Such and such a concern is weak," men say, "because its personnel lacks fidelity." *Fidelity: fidelis, faithful.*

I talked one day with a man who has seen a great many successful businesses from the inside. "You have a good opportunity for comparing men," I said. "What about these big business leaders? Wherein do they differ from others? What is the principal requisite for a man who wants to get into business for himself?"

Without a moment's hesitation he answered: "Courage to jump off the dock."

He saw that the answer was not what I had expected and so he amplified it. "That may sound strange to you," he said, "but I believe it is true. The man who can muster enough faith in a business to risk his whole future on it, to jump off the dock and sink or swim with that one proposition, he may drown, very many *do*

232

drown, but if he wins he wins big. Educated brains can be bought fairly cheap in business; muscle is a glut on the market; even energy and a certain amount of initiative can be put on the pay-roll. But real courage is rare. Hence it is the most highly rewarded quality in business life. Every big business was conceived by some one as a tremendous act of faith, and the bigger the men the bigger their belief must have been in order to lift them up to where they are."

Look about you anywhere and you find that statement verified. I once asked Henry Ford to tell me about his father, and he answered that the old gentleman had been a good citizen but timid.

"He thought I made a great mistake when I left my twenty-five dollar a week job as engineer at the electric light plant," Mr. Ford said. "He warned me that young men ought not to take such long chances. Later, when we began to build our factory, he was thoroughly scared. 'Henry, you're too late,' he exclaimed. 'By the time you get this plant finished everybody in the United States who can afford an automobile will have bought one.'"

It was in the year of the big deflation that this talk of mine with Mr. Ford took place. Rumors were flying thick and fast. It was said that Ford himself was practically bankrupt; at any moment the Wall Street banks would step in and take him over. I mentioned these stories to him.

"There are some people in this country who are a good deal worried about business," I said, "and about *your* business."

He smiled.

"What do they think? That business is going to crawl into its hole and pull the hole in after it?"

"Something like that."

"No. No," he said, shaking his head. "Business is only the mechanism for supplying human wants, and the wants keep right on getting bigger and bigger. Look what we've done in our business in the past ten years. We've put the United States on wheels. Do you suppose that people are ever going to be content to walk again? Don't you suppose that all the other people in the world are just as eager to be on wheels too? No, business won't stop. As fast as you get a want supplied a bigger want rises up to take its place."

"But about your own business," I said. "Suppose you were to go broke, would it worry you very much?"

"I think it might be interesting," he laughed.

"It would be like having two lifetimes rolled into one. And I know what I'd do; at least I know the kind of thing I'd do. I'd find something that lots of people have to have and I'd figure out some way to make it better and sell it cheaper than it's ever been made and sold before. And I'd have another fortune before I die.

"Money isn't important," he added. "I can't spend much on myself. Nobody can. A suit of clothes; a house; a car—not much that money can buy. There are only two things in the world that are really important—work and faith."

There you have the philosophy on which one of the two largest fortunes in the United States has been built. Here is a glimpse into the mind of the man who built the other. It is printed in the memoirs of the late J. I. C. Clark, who was for many years intimately associated with Standard Oil.

One day on the golf course Mr. Clark lured Mr. Rockefeller into reminiscence and finally asked him point-blank about his own private fortune. What was the secret of it? Why had he amassed so much more wealth than his associates?

WHAT CAN A MAN BELIEVE?

"He flashed a quick glance at me, his eyes closing to piercing points under a clouded brow," Mr. Clark wrote. "All his armor was on in an instant. He gazed long into my eyes and gradually his eyes widened and a look I had never seen upon his face illuminated it as he said with intense conviction 'Faith!'

" 'Faith in oil?' I said, echoing his tone.

" 'Faith in the future of oil,' he amplified. 'I first had it. I have never wavered in it. I still have it as firm as ever.

" 'Henry Rogers, he never sold a share; John D. Archbold, he was always ready to buy. Back in the 'eighties I wanted to build a house in New York, and he bought one thousand shares from me at seventy-five dollars! E. T. Bedford, when Ohio Lima Oil came in and outstunk all who tried to refine it, kept on buying until we thought he was crazy, building tanks until he had $24,-000,000 locked up in it. "Some genius," he would say, "will refine the sulphur out of it, and then——" And a genius did, and the profit was colossal. Oil for Europe, oil for Asia, oil for Africa and Australia. Faith!' Andrews, the man whose skill first made success possible, had early lost faith—and sold out—to John D."

What would have happened to history if John D. or Henry Ford had sat on the throne of Philip II of Spain? It was Philip, you remember, who determined to teach England a good lesson and so outfitted the Spanish Armada, the most powerful fleet ever gathered together up to that time. England was scared and properly so, for every advantage was on the Spanish side.

Every advantage except one. The English had Drake, who knew his business and *believed*. The Spaniards had the Duke of Medina Sidonia, who thus addressed the king:

"My health is bad and from my small experience of the water I know that I am always seasick. . . . The expedition is on such a scale and the object is of such high importance that the person at the head of it ought to understand navigation and sea fighting and I know nothing of either. . . . The Adelantado of Castile would do better than I. The Lord would help him, for he is a good Christian and has fought in naval battles. If you send me, depend upon it, I shall have a bad account to render of my trust."

He set sail expecting to fail, and he did. He had plenty of capital, plenty of men, plenty of everything but Faith.

In that same panic year when I held my conversation with Mr. Ford, I attended a convention of shoe salesmen in New York City. It was the gloomiest meeting imaginable. From every state in the Union these men had come home with stories of over-stocked shelves, cancelled orders and curt refusals to buy. They were completely whipped.

The morning session adjourned, and after a good luncheon the sales manager announced that he would like to interrupt the regular program by taking the men for a short motor ride. He loaded them into taxis and, driving down Fifth Avenue, turned into a side-street and stopped before a vacant lot. There the men were invited to get out on to the sidewalk and, wondering and grumbling, they obeyed.

"I have brought you down here," the sales manager said, "to show you this vacant lot."

One man in the rear gave forth a hoarse chuckle, and the rest looked uncertainly at one another, waiting for the joke.

"Doesn't it strike you as strange," he continued, "that right here in the very center of the richest city in the world, where land is worth thousands of dollars a foot, this fine big piece of land should be unused? There is a story here, and I shall tell it to you.

"Exactly a hundred years ago a farmer died in his farm-house which stood a few feet from where we are standing now. He left a solemn injunction in his will. His heirs might do as they pleased with the rest of his estate, but this one little section of the farm, this vacant lot, must remain forever without a building as a perpetual resting place for the bones of his wife. That, gentlemen, was just one hundred years ago, and last week the highest court of this state set aside that provision in the old man's will as being incompatible with the public interest. This vacant lot is shortly to be built upon.

"But consider for a moment the drama of it. He lived on a farm, that old man, far from the city limits. He assumed that it would be a farm always. But a few years pass, a century, less than the lifetime of three average men, and the island that was only a collection of farms becomes a city of six million people. The land that could be bought for a few dollars an acre is worth thousands of dollars a foot. Where there were chicken coops and pastures there are skyscrapers towering forty stories into the sky. And all in a hundred years.

"You are going back to your different territories," the sales manager continued, "back to the merchants who act as though the United States were bankrupt, as though business will never recover, as though the people of the country will never again need any more shoes or clothes or houses or automobiles. And I want you to carry with you a mental photograph of this vacant lot. I want you to tell those merchants about it. I want you to say to them: 'We are living in a country that was only farms a hundred years ago and is now the richest country in the world. And it has only started. Nothing can stop it; nothing can prevent an active, intelligent man from prospering in it except his own lack of vision. Nothing except the same short-sightedness which made this old farmer believe that, because his land had always been a farm, it would continue to be always. That sort of thinking will keep any man poor. But no man can fail to make progress if, in spite of the little ups and downs of business, he keeps his faith in the United States."

For a common, every-day business man it was a pretty good little oration. It is the creed of the men who have built big things. They do not buy bonds; they buy common stocks in order to share in the growth of the country. They have their set-backs, their periods of retrenchment, sometimes periods when their enthusiasm leads them too far and punishes them with a fall. But through thick and thin they stick to their faith that the country must go forward; and in that faith they win.

It goes without saying that they have a vital faith in themselves as well. The man who lacks that is in a sad way indeed.

MAGIC THAT MOVES MOUNTAINS

Some years ago a crumpled and dejected citizen came to my office, and slumped down into a chair. I knew him by name. He had been for several years the sales manager of a small but profitable company in the Middle West, and had established some reputation as a writer of effective sales literature. In broken sentences, heavy with despair, he proceeded to tell his story. His salary in the little town where he lived had been small but it was sufficient to give him a place in the community. His only child was grown, and he and his wife had assumed that they were securely settled for life. One day there came to him a persuasive individual of the promoter type, offering him the unheard-of sum of fifteen thousand dollars a year to move to New York. Our friend was staggered by the offer and quite unwilling to believe that he could ever earn so much; but the promoter prevailed upon him finally and, with much misgivings, he resigned his job, sold his home, and made the move.

For six months everything went smoothly. He had a nice office and the title of vice-president; he was beginning to believe that his dream was really true when suddenly the concern blew up and the promoter-president vanished. Our man was completely dazed. Never in his whole business experience had he been separated one single week from a Saturday night pay envelope. The prospect filled his soul with terror. He was ready to take any sort of a job, anything at any salary, no matter how little. Failing to find immediate employment, he was almost in a frame of mind to throw himself into the river.

"You are in a very unhappy situation," I said, when he had finished his sad story.

He nodded dejectedly.

"It is a very serious situation," I mentioned, "on one condition."

"On what condition?" he repeated dully.

"On condition that you have been making your living all these years under false pretenses. That you really can't write sales letters."

He straightened up.

"But I can write sales letters," he exclaimed.

"That's the stuff," I answered. "That's the first really worthy remark you have made this afternoon. If it is true, you have nothing to fear. Come here a minute."

I led him over to the window.

"Look out there at those buildings," I said. "All filled with offices. Business offices. Offices of people who have goods to sell and most of whom don't know how to sell them. Have you money enough to live on for sixty days even if nothing comes in?"

He nodded. He had been thrifty.

"Then do this. Go down to a good printer and get yourself a letterhead. Use your apartment for your office for the present. It will do until you get something better. Take the classified telephone directory and pick out the names of a hundred concerns that have something to sell to the public. You say you can write a sales letter. This is your great chance to prove it. Write those people a letter that will sell them the idea that they need you to help them sell their goods. And if they ask for a reference, tell them to telephone me."

He went out of the office with the first little gleam of faith in himself. From time to time during the next few weeks he dropped in to report progress. At the end of the first six months he told me that his earnings were running at the rate of more than twenty-five thousand dollars a year. It was the nearest thing to a miracle that has ever taken place under my own observation, the raising from the dead of a man through the sheer lifting power of faith in himself.

If you go to a town in Colorado, which we shall call Erewhon, though it can not be found on the map under that name, you will see a very large smelting plant and a group of other buildings that constitute the principal industry of the town, affording employment to several hundred people and feeding more than half the families. And you will learn that it does not work in gold or silver or copper, but in a particular product made from what was formerly counted a waste stratum that came out inevitably with the ore that the miners sought. They will tell you that this stratum, more valuable than the ore itself, would still have been waste had not Old Man August Bender made a fortunate discovery twenty-five years ago, just about the time when the mines themselves were shutting down.

August Bender had been educated at Heidelberg, and when the stein was on the table and the good song ringing clear, he was among the participants. The song died out, but the stein remained his companion. Migrating to America and eventually to Colorado, he was out of work, out at the elbows, out of money, and in debt. There came a home missionary preacher to that town, and he had to make up his church membership out of the odds and ends and leavings of civilization's backwash. He had as church clerk a careless boy who blotted the books and neglected his business. One day the preacher chanced to see some of August Bender's handwriting and discovered in him a character that gave him faith in this man of the gutter. He made August the church clerk.

There was great glee in the leading saloon over this appointment, and some wondered whether August would be sober enough on Sunday to attend service. He was, and, to the credit of those men, they did not tempt him to be otherwise. When Sunday came August cleaned and pressed his shabby suit and went to church. The church books from that date were kept immaculate. And August Bender was one of the most faithful attendants at every meeting.

To be sure, he still had occasional sprees. As long as he lived he was sometimes a little the worse for liquor. But gradually the periods of sobriety lengthened as he began to gain confidence and self-respect through the preacher's confidence in him; and as the community saw him making a heroic fight they tried to help him. Even the ungodly wanted August Bender to win.

Under this new lease of self-respect and a new birth of faith, August obtained a position as secretary of a sporadic mine. The organization had little capital and did not last long. August saw it peter out.

But he began experimenting with the waste rock that lay in the ore. He got a blow-pipe and a crucible and worked half secretly on something no one understood.

One day he called together his employers and a few others and showed them three letters. One was from Denver, one from Washington, and one from Heidelberg. All three agreed that he had found a deposit rich in something of real value and that it would be profitable provided it did not cost too much to get it out. That point was already settled; August had found the way to extract it.

A new company was organized, with August Bender as secretary. It took over a number of shut-down plants, and the stock began paying dividends from the start.

August Bender is dead, but he died respected and he died decently. His widow is still living and, while not rich, has abundant provision for her needs in the stock he left her in the company. His son has his father's place as secretary, and besides his salary owns a good block of stock. The company flourishes, and so does the town. They are building a new church in that town just now, and the company of which we are speaking is making a liberal donation toward it.

"We can afford it," said the manager of the company. "If the preacher back there twenty-five years ago had not had faith in God and

August Bender the railroad company would have pulled up its sidetracks, and this town would have moved off the map."

It would be easy to multiply such stories. Every business man knows some of the same sort; every preacher has seen them in his own experience. They merely pile up the proof of what we have been saying. A man can lose everything—his fortune, his standing in the community, even his own self-respect—and still win his way back to success, provided only that one single human being still has faith in him.

Faith in business, faith in the country, faith in one's self, faith in other people—this is the power that moves the world. And why is it unreasonable to believe that this power, which is so much stronger than any other, is merely a fragment of the Great Power which operates the universe?

One of the most tragic incidents in history was the return of Jesus to His home town. He had slipped away from the carpenter shop some months earlier to begin His public work, and marvelous stories of His success had drifted back. He had healed sick people in Capernaum. He had fed hungry people. He had raised the dead. He had preached to great crowds. He had held His own in public debate with the shrewdest minds. There was a stir of curiosity at the report that He was coming back.

And He Himself must have felt a thrill at the prospect. If He could do these wonderful things in unfamiliar places what might He not do in His own town, among the people who had known Him all His life? There were sick, old neighbors to whom He could give health. There were hungry people with whom He could share His bounty. There were puzzled, tired, hopeless people to whom He could give the words of eternal hope. Full of enthusiasm and self-confidence He walked up the street and entered the synagogue.

And there a shock awaited Him. He looked down into those faces which should have been filled with pride and belief, and found what? Cynicism. Doubt. The sneering complacency of the small-town mind. They were not going to be fooled, these wise ones. They knew Him. A prophet, was He? That might go in Capernaum where He was unknown, but *they* knew Him. He was no prophet; He was just a boy who had grown up among them. Just Jesus, the carpenter's son. So they waited contemptuously, daring Him to perform His miracles, taunting Him with their cynical smiles.

And a tragic thing happened.

MAGIC THAT MOVES MOUNTAINS

The power that had healed sick people and raised the dead was impotent. The great urge that was in Him to do something splendid for these people could not express itself. He stood there, He who believed that all the forces of the Almighty were at His command, and could achieve no result. "He could do there no mighty work," says the record, "because of their unbelief." Because they were sure that nothing fine was going to happen to them, nothing did happen. Because they could not stretch out even a little way toward Him, He could not reach them. A woman in another town could touch only the hem of His garment to be cured. A mother could cry: "Lord, Lord," and receive her son back from the grave. A Centurion could say: "Only speak the word and my daughter shall live again." These miracles were easy. But His own people could have nothing—*because of their unbelief.*

Since faith will do so much, and the lack of it is so destroying, why not believe? What does one lose by accepting the positive side of the argument and acting on its impulse? What can one lose that is anything in comparison with the gain?

Granting again the strongest possible case that can be brought against the record of the church, does it not still merit the united effort of honest men to help it work out its more effective future? Remember if you will the Dark Ages, with their corruption, ignorance and superstition. But remember also a noble hymnology; an ascendant art; a glorious architecture; a ritual impressive and adapted to all the manifold needs of life; the church present at the cradle with baptism; present at puberty with confirmation; present at the wedding and establishment of the new home; present at the grave. Every momentous occasion dignified and lifted by its blessing and belief.

Remember the fall of Rome when government went, art went, everything went except the church. It conquered the barbarian conquerors, and, standing firm, kept civilization from the scrap heap. Remember Columbus planting in America the Cross, sign of a Catholic Church. Remember Jesuit missionaries exploring these unknown lands and giving to our rivers Indian names in French mispronunciation. Heroic men, eager to save human souls; teaching the savages—so the Rev. John Williams says in the *Redeemed Captive*—to baptize babies before scalping them. Crude men but strong, thrust forward by faith and leaving imprints because of the power of their belief.

And then remember the thousands of churches to-day, few of them led by great men but all served by earnest men and all, however faintly, holding up the torch of order and organization, and a sense of decency and righteousness.

Holding fast to their faith in the eternal importance of human life and its continuance beyond the grave. Expressing that faith often in very ghastly funeral services, yet expressing it none the less. Saying to men: "This earthly life which you know now is only an intermediate stage in a threefold life. Every one of you has lived before, and for ten lunar months possessed a life continuous with that which you now possess. It was not possible for you *then* to know anything about this present phase of life; it would be strange if now you were allowed to know very much about the life that is to be. But once already you have passed through darkness and pain and emerged into a bright new world. So shall you emerge again. Believe and you shall live."

Does not this record and this faith confer power and dignity on human life? Is not the church, as the one channel through which faith has been steadily transmitted, worthy of a determined effort for its strengthening and betterment on the part of all? It has seemed so to me, and out of that conviction has come this little book. The book began with an anecdote and with another it ends.

The great fire of 1666 destroyed the central part of London and laid a large number of its churches in ruins. It completely gutted the old St. Paul's and made necessary the building of the present noble cathedral. This was the opportunity for Sir Christopher Wren, to whom London owes very much for what is finest in its architecture and especially in the character of its central churches. He received for his compensation a salary less than that of the American unskilled worker, but as his epitaph truly says, his work was "not for his own but for the public good," and will keep bright his fame forever.

One morning he passed among the workmen, most of whom did not know him, and of three different men engaged in the same kind of work he asked the same question: "What are you doing?" From the first he received the answer: "I am cutting this stone." From the second the answer was: "I am earning three shillings and six pence a day." But the third man straightened up, squared his shoulders, and holding his mallet in one hand and chisel in the other, proudly replied: "I am helping Sir

Christopher Wren to build this great cathedral."

These are the three ways of looking at life:

1. I am just cutting this stone.
2. I am only earning a living.
3. I am doing a small part of a great work.

I have not seen the Architect and I do not altogether understand the plan. But I believe there *is* a plan, so I work with good spirit in which is no fear.

THE END